SHAKESPEARE'S LAST PLAYS

Shakespeare's Last Plays

E. M. W. TILLYARD

LITT. D., F.B.A

Late Master of Jesus College
Cambridge

1968

CHATTO AND WINDUS

LONDON

Published by
Chatto & Windus Ltd
42 William IV Street
London W.C.2

*

Clarke, Irwin & Co Ltd
Toronto

First Published 1938
Second Impression 1951
Third Impression 1954
Fourth Impression 1958
Fifth Impression 1962
Sixth Impression 1964
Seventh Impression 1968

SBN 7011 1158 5

Printed in Great Britain by
Lowe & Brydone (Printers) Ltd
London

CONTENTS

PREFACE

THE gist of the following pages was delivered as a lecture at the Sorbonne in the spring of 1936. It was later expanded into three lectures for the English Faculty at Cambridge. In putting it into book form I have tried to recast it, but some traces of lecture-technique may have remained against my will. Should they do so, the reader may resent them the less, if he understands how they came to be there.

It is difficult, in guessing at Shakespeare's intentions when he wrote his plays, to avoid the error of describing those intentions as if they were very deliberate, as if he had planned everything out in careful abstract before-hand. If I have fallen into this error, it was in order to save words, and I wish to repudiate it except as a means of brevity, of temporary convenience.

E. M. W. T.

I. INTRODUCTORY

HOWEVER sharply the critics disagree in interpreting *Cymbeline*, *The Winter's Tale*, and *The Tempest*, they are at one in this: that these plays are mutually connected with an intimacy different from that connecting any three either of the earlier comedies or of the tragedies. *As You Like It* is self-supporting; we do not require the help of *Much Ado* to understand it. Similarly we need not refer to *Othello* in order to understand *Macbeth*. But the prospect of understanding *Cymbeline* without *The Winter's Tale* and *The Tempest* is poor indeed. And even *The Tempest*, usually thought the most successful of the three, gains much in lucidity when supported by the others.

Coming to the reason of this intimate connection, we find not perhaps unanimity but a fairly strong trend of opinion. Shakespeare, it is said, was feeling his way, was experimenting, in a manner quite alien to *Much Ado* or *Othello*. He fumbled in *Cymbeline*, did better in *The Winter's Tale*, and only in his third attempt achieved full success.

It is when they reach the question what Shakespeare was trying to do that critics seriously begin their habitual wranglings. We are told on the one hand that in his final phase Shakespeare had become religious and attempted to render a mystical conception of the universe; we are told on the other that he ended his days in boredom, cynicism, and disillusion, and that the technique of verse was all that remained in life to interest him. Other critics, less avid of the vast generalisation, see Shakespeare, the tempestuous adventure of the Dark Lady forgotten, doting with benevolent purity on his now mature young daughter under the successive forms of Marina, Imogen, Perdita, and Miranda, paying a compliment to his medical son-in-law, Dr. Hall, in the character of Cornelius in *Cymbeline*, or even counselling the youthful Fletcher, through the lesson in lumbering imposed on Ferdinand, to take more pains with his plays.

Before having my own say, I will review one or two general criticisms. First there is Lytton Strachey's, stated in extreme form above, that Shakespeare was bored. Perhaps it was echoed by Granville-Barker, who noted in *Cymbeline* a certain sophistication of artifice:

> This art that displays art is a thing very likely to be to the taste of the mature and rather wearied artist. When you are exhausted with hammering great tragic themes into shape it is a relief to find a subject you can play with.

But this acute and temperate comment on a single play is remote from Strachey's imputation of weariness to the whole group:

> It is difficult to resist the conclusion that Shakespeare was getting bored himself. Bored with people, bored with real life, bored with drama, bored, in fact, with everything except poetry and poetical dreams. He is no longer interested, one often feels, in what happens, or who says what, so long as he can find place for a faultless lyric, or a new, unimagined rhythmical effect, or a grand and mystic speech.

2

INTRODUCTORY

Strachey's essay was published in 1906, and it was a timely rebuke to the vision, popular enough at that date, of Shakespeare 'on the heights,' wrapped in the impenetrable mantle of his own virtue, watching with godlike serenity the happy issue which he was now confident the passionate struggles of mankind must ultimately have. But as positive criticism Strachey's essay is at complete odds with my strongest convictions about the plays. There is no lack of vitality, Shakespeare is not bored with things; and my conviction of this springs from the rhythms, the imagery, in fact from those most intimate poetical qualities about which it is futile to argue. Middleton Murry is right when he says that even in the least congenial of the three plays, *Cymbeline*, 'the verse is sinewy from first to last: manifestly the work of a poet in whom the faculty was at height.' As to Shakespeare's remoteness from real life and his preoccupation with 'grand and mystic speeches,' consider this passage, which follows the grandest and most mysterious of all the speeches in Shakespeare's last plays. After Prospero has pronounced that we are such stuff as dreams are made on, he calls Ariel, who reports as follows on the conspirators, Stephano, Trinculo, and Caliban:

> I told you, sir, they were red-hot with drinking;
> So full of valour that they smote the air
> For breathing in their faces; beat the ground
> For kissing of their feet; yet always bending
> Towards their project. Then I beat my tabor;
> At which, like unback'd colts, they prick'd their ears,
> Advanced their eyelids, lifted up their noses
> As they smelt music: so I charm'd their ears,
> That calf-like they my lowing follow'd through

3

Tooth'd briers, sharp furzes, pricking goss, and thorns,
Which entered their frail shins: at last I left them
I' the filthy-mantled pool beyond your cell,
There dancing up to the chins, that the foul lake
O'erstunk their feet.

Shakespeare focusses all his attention on this description. He is entirely engrossed in his drunkards, who plainly are very drunk indeed, as genuinely and positively drunk as any men in a play can be. Not only does Ariel's speech refute Lytton Strachey, but it supplies in its realism a contrast to Prospero's late mysterious utterance that can hardly be accidental. But here I begin to anticipate, and must turn to the second notion I wish to review.

Some have made much of the theatrical conditions of the time, and have seen in them the reason why Shakespeare introduced certain changes into his last plays. First, there was the shift of setting from the Globe Theatre to the Blackfriars, from the open air to an indoor theatre. Shakespeare, with the opportunism that always marked his stage career, could not possibly have remained indifferent to the change. The indoor theatres, with their candlelight and with facilities of vision little affected by the weather, were suited to masque and pageantry; while their enclosedness and the good behaviour of the audience[1] encouraged delicacy of intonation rather than shouting. Thus, in that they may well have prompted Shakespeare to use certain materials, they should be taken into account. Yet his resilience was such, and his power of getting different results from the same materials was so great, that theatrical conditions could dictate only

[1] See J. Isaacs, *Production and Stage-Management at the Blackfriars Theatre* (Shakespeare Association Pamphlet, 1933), pp. 5-6.

in a very limited degree the emotional effect he was to produce. When all has been said about them, the main business of criticism remains to be transacted.

Secondly, there was the rising popularity of Shakespeare's juniors, Beaumont and Fletcher. It was once usual to overestimate their influence on Shakespeare's last plays, now rather to ignore it. Critics used to argue something like this: There are qualities in the last plays new in Shakespeare. For instance, never before was he so shameless in creating, against all probability, a melodramatic situation for just that situation's sake. That Imogen may be in the strange case of waking to find what seems her husband's headless body beside her, she herself must be given (by roundabout means) a drug with most unusual properties; Cloten must procure a suit of Posthumus's clothes; must undertake alone a journey on which in all likelihood he would have been accompanied; and, most strange of all, must, head apart, sufficiently resemble the peerless Posthumus in figure to pass for him in the eyes of his wife. All this improbable apparatus Shakespeare puts up with that Imogen may be able to match a big speech to the melodramatic situation. Now such an easy artistic conscience in manipulating a scene is the consistent mark of Beaumont and Fletcher, in whom (to quote the modern writer who has written best about them [1]) 'it is the situation or emotional crisis that is preserved, while the motivation shows unmistakable signs of patching.' Now, if this subservience of motivation to emotional crisis is both new in Shakespeare and habitual in Beaumont and Fletcher, Shakespeare must have derived it from them. Turning to *Philaster* and

[1] U. M. Ellis-Fermor, *The Jacobean Drama* (1936), p. 207.

5

Cymbeline, which cannot be many years apart in date, the critics noted a number of resemblances and concluded that Shakespeare wrote with Beaumont and Fletcher's play as his model. And even if he went far beyond them in *The Winter's Tale* and *The Tempest*, it was they who supplied him with the fantasies and the improbabilities that separate his last plays from those that preceded them.

The weakness of the above supposition is that we know too little of the dates of Beaumont and Fletcher's plays to be certain that the influence was from them on Shakespeare rather than the other way round. Most of their tragedies and tragi-comedies come after *Cymbeline*, and even *Philaster* may easily do so. Thus the more cautious scholars retorted; and their opposition suited another trend of opinion. Ever since Rupert Brooke described Fletcher's tragic work as a 'sea of saccharine,' people have been apprehensive lest they should like it too well, and hence have tended to leave it alone. They were glad to learn that the old supposition was not very securely based, and dismissed it from their minds, relieved that they could, with a good conscience, clear Shakespeare of the least taint of saccharine. The question of Beaumont and Fletcher's influence on Shakespeare has, in fact, been warehoused rather than disposed of for good.

An unprejudiced reader can hardly avoid admitting the probability that Shakespeare was very much aware of Beaumont and Fletcher indeed. Even if *Philaster* came after *Cymbeline*, there remains *The Faithful Shepherdess*, while in the close and eager world of theatrical alliances and rivalries it must have been known what Beaumont and Fletcher were good at, quite apart from any plays

6

that have come down to us. *The Faithful Shepherdess* comes just before Shakespeare's final period. Though it stands a little away from the normal drama in being a pastoral and in being written mainly in couplets, yet it is a tragi-comedy as regards plot, and it exhibits two of Fletcher's most characteristic and constant qualities. These are, a mellifluousness of verse, which in the year 1608 must have been new and fascinating, and a technique that sacrificed (if need be) all else to neatness of plot and the unrelated sensational situation. Seeing that Shakespeare was susceptible to changes of literary taste, that he was modest and wrote in humble terms a sonnet about a poet inferior to himself ('Was it the proud full sail of his great verse?'), that at any time a poet is apt to overestimate some of his contemporaries (as T. S. Eliot has overestimated Ezra Pound, and W. B. Yeats several poets represented in *The Oxford Book of Modern Verse*), we shall be flying in the face of common sense if we deny the likelihood of Shakespeare's being greatly impressed by the brilliant innovations of these two clever and well-bred young dramatists. Is it likely, for instance, that Shakespeare should have remained unmoved by the scene in *The Faithful Shepherdess* where, through misunderstanding, Perigot sets out to murder his beloved Amoret? Here is Amoret's liquid rhetoric, in which she protests:

> Can there be any age, or days, or time,
> Or tongues of men, guilty so great a crime
> As wronging simple maid? Oh, Perigot,
> Thou that wast yesterday without a blot;
> Thou that wast every good and every thing
> That men call blessed; thou that wast the spring

From whence our looser grooms drew all their best;
Thou that wast always just and always blest
In faith and promise; thou that hadst the name
Of virtuous given thee, and made good the same
Even from thy cradle; thou that wast that all
That men delighted in! Oh, what a fall
Is this, to have been so, and now to be
The only best in wrong and infamy!
And I to live to know this! and by me,
That lov'd thee dearer than mine eyes, or that
Which we esteem'd our honour, virgin-state!
Dearer than swallows love the early morn,
Or dogs of chase the sound of merry horn;
Dearer than thou canst love thy new love, if thou hast
Another, and far dearer than the last;
Dearer than thou canst love thyself, though all
The self-love were within thee that did fall
With that coy swain that now is made a flower,
For whose dear sake Echo weeps many a shower!
And am I thus rewarded for my flame?
Loved worthily to get a wanton's name?
Come, thou forsaken willow, wind my head,
And noise it to the world, my love is dead!
I am forsaken, I am cast away,
And left for every lazy groom to say
I was unconstant, light, and sooner lost
Than the quick clouds we see, or the chill frost
When the hot sun beats on it! Tell me yet,
Canst thou not love again thy Amoret?

That it is now fashionable to call such verse escapist
does not in the least alter the overwhelming effect it must
have had, when new, on other verse-practitioners. Its
very slickness would dazzle (at least at first) and divert

men's eyes from faults which to us show up clearly enough. It is most probable that Fletcher's verse encouraged Shakespeare to introduce every now and then a new style of stillness and sweetness into his last plays, for instance, in some of the speeches of Belarius and the two youths in the Welsh mountains in *Cymbeline*, and in the statue scene in *The Winter's Tale*. As to Fletcher's method of manipulating melodramatic scenes for their own sake in isolation, Shakespeare may well have used it experimentally in *Cymbeline*, as in Imogen's waking beside the headless Cloten, referred to above.

That Shakespeare followed Fletcher does not in the least mean that he resembled Fletcher in final poetic effect. Here, as ever, Shakespeare transformed an alien suggestion into something entirely his own. The general process can be illustrated by the way he adapts a single passage. Bellario in *Philaster*, astray in the forest, favours the flowers with a confidential soliloquy:

> Bear me, thou gentle bank,
> For ever, if thou wilt. You sweet ones all,
> Let me unworthy press you: I could wish
> I rather were a corse strewed o'er with you
> Than quick above you.

Perdita in *The Winter's Tale*, after speaking of the spring flowers, says to her guests and to Florizel:

> O, these I lack
> To make you garlands of, and my sweet friend,
> To strew him o'er and o'er!
> *Flo.*   What, like a corse?
> *Per.* No, like a bank for love to lie and play on;
> Not like a corse; or if, not to be buried,
> But quick and in mine arms.

9

The verbal echoes are too close to be fortuitous; and if, as is likely, Shakespeare was writing after Fletcher, he has transformed something thin and sweet into something so rich as to be scarcely comparable with its original. Miss Ellis-Fermor [1] (who recognises Shakespeare's debt to Beaumont and Fletcher) puts the general process well enough:

> By one of those paradoxes which this drama continually offers us, Shakespeare used for the culminating expression of his faith in reality that form which its inventors had devised as a means of escape. The fairy-tale with him becomes charged with those implications which the more immediate types of story could not present, becomes the vehicle of imaginative experience and interprets the real world more truly than do the records of actuality.

But though it is wrong to ignore Beaumont and Fletcher, it is equally wrong to suppose that the things Shakespeare derived from them were exclusively their property. On the contrary, behind them all was a stock of romantic incident, the common property of the early Jacobean age.[2] This stock was partly medieval and partly classical, a fantastic medley of those medieval romances (like *Huon of Bordeaux*, source of Shakespeare's Oberon) which had remained popular and of the late Greek romances. It was from this stock that Spenser drew much of his material for *The Fairy Queen*, but its great rehandling in its usual form of prose narrative was Sidney's *Arcadia*. We shall not understand what Shakespeare's contemporaries expected from the romantic

---

[1] *Op. cit.*, p. 268.
[2] See E. K. Chambers, *Shakespeare: a Survey*, p. 288.

material and what types of feeling they thought it
capable of treating, unless we remember what they
thought of *Arcadia*.

There is a general reluctance to-day to allow much
weight to any Elizabethan literature outside the drama
and the lyric. It is as easy to persuade five people to
read Webster as to persuade one to read Spenser. And
the number of people who have read *Arcadia* for pleasure
must be very small. This reluctance is at hopeless odds
with Elizabethan taste and critical opinion. If any book
then combined in the highest degree delight with instruc-
tion, it was *Arcadia*. This vast prose romance was
immensely popular, probably on account of its rich and
vital style and of its wealth of romantic incident; it was
also highly esteemed by the learned as a true prose epic
on the model of Heliodorus's *Ethiopica*. By presenting
examples of heroic virtue to be imitated and eminent
vice to be shunned, it fulfilled the moral requirements of
the Renaissance epic, while it abounded in political
wisdom drawn from Machiavelli and was possibly illustrated by topical reference. Further, there was a strong
classical tinge. The plot was conducted on the tradi-
tional lines of the classical epic, with the action opening
in the middle—the shipwreck of two unknown young
men—and the early part narrated episodically. The
battles are strongly reminiscent of the *Aeneid*, and the
whole action is motivated by the Aristotelian frailty of
the Arcadian king, Basilius, who, though mainly good,
will not rest content with present fair fortune but insists
on consulting oracles about his future. It thus happened
that Sidney in writing *Arcadia* not only gave the romantic
material a new popularity but, by treating this material

with such academic correctness, immensely raised the whole status of the romance in the eyes of the Elizabethans and Jacobeans. The notion, so widespread to-day, that Elizabethan drama dealt with life while Elizabethan romance escaped from it, is as alien to Elizabethan opinion as it should prove itself false to any modern who troubles to read *Arcadia* with sympathetic attention.

When, therefore, Shakespeare began using romantic material at the end of his career instead of Holinshed and Plutarch, it was not necessarily because he wanted to 'escape' or to be less serious. The 'feigned' history he chose to draw on was taken quite as seriously by his contemporaries as the true history he abandoned. It is through forgetting the place of *Arcadia* in Elizabethan thought that Schücking writes in this strain about the character of Ferdinand in *The Tempest*: [1]

> Still less of colour and life is there in Ferdinand's portrait. He may be said to be almost entirely lacking in personal traits. He is the model of the noble cavalier. It is characteristic of him that the first expression that crosses his lips upon espying the mistress of the island is a request to be told how he has to behave in this place. His mind is bent upon proper behaviour. Honour, piety, and the service of his mistress fill his chivalrous heart.

This formality of Ferdinand is acutely noted and well described, yet the implication of Schücking's total description, that Shakespeare is not being very serious in drawing Ferdinand, is quite wrong. When Ferdinand meets Miranda for the first time and says:

[1] *Character Problems in Shakespeare's Plays*, pp. 246-7.

INTRODUCTORY

> Most sure, the goddess
> On whom these airs attend! Vouchsafe, my prayer
> May know if you remain upon this island;
> And that you will some good instruction give
> How I may bear me here,

he should be approximated to the courtly setting of *Arcadia*, where correctness of manners was of prime importance. Ferdinand's anxiety to know how to behave reminds me of Amphialus's anxiety to wear the right clothes for courting Philoclea, whom he holds captive :

> But Amphialus (taking of his mother Philoclea's knives, which he kept as a relic since she had worn them) got up, and, calling for his richest apparel, nothing seemed sumptuous enough for his mistress's eyes: and that which was costly he feared was not dainty; and though the invention were delicate, he misdoubted the making. As careful he was too of the colour; lest, if gay, he might seem to glory in his injury and her wrong; if mourning, it might strike some evil presage unto her of her fortune. At length he took a garment more rich than glaring, the ground being black velvet richly embroidered with great pearl and precious stones, but they set so among certain tuffs of cypress that the cypress was like black clouds, through which the stars might yield a dark lustre. About his neck he wore a broad and gorgeous collar: whereof the pieces interchangeably answering, the one was of diamonds and pearl set with a white enamel, so that by the cunning of the workman it seemed like a shining ice; and the other piece, being of rubies and opals, had a fiery glistering, which he thought pictured the two passions of fear and desire, wherein he was enchained. His hurt, not yet fully well, made him a little halt, but he strove to give the best grace he could unto his halting.
>
> And in that sort he went to Philoclea's chamber.

This is an extremely serious passage, an example of

the immense importance of all kinds of heraldry, symbolism, emblematic writing in the Renaissance world; and it is a gross error in ourselves if we merely enjoy it as quaint. And so with Ferdinand and the whole world of Elizabethan romance for which he stands. They may not be to our taste, but they were very much a part of life in early Jacobean days.

To sum up my review of what Shakespeare owed to contemporary conditions in the theatre, we see him taking up technical hints from the indoor theatre and from two rising young dramatists and paying added heed to the world of romance typified in *Arcadia* and consistently popular with his contemporaries, the dramatists included. In doing all these things, however, there is no suspicion that he did not mainly do what he wanted, turning borrowed matter to his own ends. And the question remains: What were those ends?

The third type of criticism I have to review, the notion that in his last plays Shakespeare made a new start, will lead naturally to the first section of my own remarks. Lytton Strachey postulated a complete break between *Antony and Cleopatra* and all the last plays from *Coriolanus* on. E. K. Chambers [1] conjectures nothing less than a religious conversion or a nervous breakdown between the tragedies and the romances:

> The profound cleavage in Shakespeare's mental history about 1607-1608 must have been due to some spiritual crisis the nature of which it is only possible dimly to conjecture; some such process as that which in the psychology of religion bears the name of conversion; or perhaps some sickness of the brain

[1] *Op. cit.*, p. 293.

which left him an old man, freed at last from the fever of speculation and well disposed to spend the afternoon of life in unexacting and agreeable dreams. This latter hypothesis would help also to explain the marked change of style which accompanies the change of dramatic purpose in the romances. In these complicated and incoherent periods, in these softened and unaccentuated rhythms, in these tender and evanescent beauties, I find less a deliberate attempt to reduce the declamation of the stage to the colloquial dialogue of daily life, than the natural outcome of relaxed mental energies, shrinking from the effort after the wrought and nervous rhythms of the past.

The change or breakdown took place, he thinks, between *Timon* (which he dates very late, after the Roman plays) and *Pericles*. As it is precisely the opposite notion I have to develop, namely, that the romances supplement the tragedies, I will leave the above quotation and speak for myself.

II. THE TRAGIC PATTERN

i. Introductory

I BEGIN with a certain conception of tragedy. In recent talk about tragedy, two conceptions have stood out in strong opposition the one to the other. The first is the stoical. In this view, tragedy is concerned with resistance to circumstance. Through the nature of things, man at his highest can only resist the forces of the universe; he cannot co-operate with them. His courage is the saving virtue in an incurably perverse state of affairs. The other conception, though it can include a measure of stoical resistance, includes some sort of reconciliation in the full tragic pattern. Man is summoned to resist certain things in the universal scheme, and suffering and loss result. But ultimately he is reconciled. There is reconstruction after disintegration. And it is precisely this sense of renewal that accounts for the peculiar tonic effect of the greatest tragedy. Mr. F. L. Lucas represents the stoical view when he writes:

> Tragedy is man's answer to the universe which crushes him so pitilessly. Destiny scowls upon him: his answer is to sit down and paint her where she stands.

Such a definition may fit Webster: it does not correspond to what I feel about *Othello*. That play does something more than picture with unflinching courage and accuracy a number of people crushed by the universe. It pictures through the hero not only the destruction of an established way of life, but the birth of a new order. Othello in his final soliloquy is a man of a more capacious mind than the Othello who first meets us. Dover Wilson has the same feeling about Shakespearean tragedy when he says:

The Lear that dies is not a Lear defiant, but a Lear redeemed. His education is complete, his regeneration accomplished.

True, the new order is cut short in both plays, but its creation is an essential part of the tragic pattern. Of the conception of tragedy as destruction followed by regeneration there have been many elaborations. Miss Maud Bodkin, in her *Archetypal Patterns in Poetry*, gives one of the most interesting. Although she writes as a psychologist and treats the subject with subtlety and complexity, she presents us with a theory which can be put in the simplest terms of everyday speech and can be applied to the most general human experiences. Indeed, it fits one of the most elementary life-processes, one so simple and obvious as to be almost embarrassing to mention. All growth implies destruction and re-creation. Any important mental growth implies them very markedly; they are jointly inherent in any vital change. Thus it is that the man is most alive who is the readiest to forgo the lazy comforts of his own habitual ways of thinking, and, when confronted with a new situation, to recast the contents of his mind. Such a recasting is invariably painful, although it brings its reward. Tragedy symbolises this process; and those who witness tragedy are encouraged to heighten their own vitality by re-enacting the same process in themselves. In this sense tragedy goes outside drama. It is to be found in the last book of the *Iliad* and in

17

Lycidas, as well as in Shakespearean tragedy. Put in these very simple terms, the notion of tragedy as implying regeneration may commend itself to some who might object to it in a more dogmatic or moral form. Anyhow, I postulate some such notion for my present purposes.

Othello is typical of Shakespearean tragedy in merely hinting at a rebirth. The complete tragic pattern is to be found in the Aeschylean trilogy. Here the evidence is that the first two plays dealt with the destructive process, the last with new creation. The *Eumenides*, the only third play that survives as a whole, records the beginning of a new way of life after the destructive havoc wrought by the old blood-feud. And the final, lost, play of the Promethean trilogy represented a new order of things when Prometheus was reconciled with Zeus. Even after the practice of staging a connected trilogy was abandoned, a play could still deal wholly or in part with the theme of rebirth. Sophocles's *Oedipus at Colonus* is wholly concerned with this theme, the previous destruction being taken for granted. Euripides's *Hercules Furens*, a very long play, resembles a compressed trilogy. It deals with Heracles's triumph, his madness and humiliation when he kills his children, and his revival at the end through the good offices of Theseus.

Moreover, when Shakespeare was writing a series of connected plays, he showed that he was aware of the complete tragic pattern, even though he did not then come to complete it. From *Richard II*, the two *Henry IVs*, and *Henry V*, it is clear that Shakespeare, like his contemporaries, looked on the course of English history from the days of Edward III to the establishment of the Tudors as first a fair state of things, then the balance of that state

upset, then a terrible period of uncertainty and suffering
(punctuated, it is true, by a short period of anticipatory
prosperity), and finally, issuing from the suffering, an
even fairer state than had existed in the beginning. In
Richard II special stress is laid on the original prosperity,
on Edward III and his seven sons. In the second scene
of the play the Duchess of Gloucester, speaking to John
of Gaunt, thus describes this prosperity:

> Edward's seven sons, whereof thyself art one,
> Were as seven vials of his sacred blood,
> Or seven fair branches springing from one root.

But this prosperity was upset by a crime; and the Duchess
continues:

> Some of those seven are dried by nature's course,
> Some of those branches by the Destinies cut;
> But Thomas, my dear lord, my life, my Gloucester,
> One vial full of Edward's sacred blood,
> One flourishing branch of his most royal root,
> Is crack'd, and all the precious liquor spilt,
> Is hack'd down, and his summer leaves all faded,
> By envy's hand and murder's bloody axe.

And in the first scene Bolingbroke describes how the
murderer of Gloucester—

> Sluiced out his innocent soul through streams of blood;
> Which blood, like sacrificing Abel's, cries,
> Even from the tongueless caverns of the earth,
> To me for justice and rough chastisement.

From this crime follows a worse: the murder of the
King, whose ghost haunts his successor and the thought
of whom troubles even the righteous King, Henry V, on

the eve of Agincourt. Having queered his own pitch by his immature historical plays, Shakespeare chose not to complete the pattern by describing the Wars of the Roses and the establishment of the Tudors. He contented himself with inserting a few hints of future prosperity in *Henry V*. The Welsh valour of Fluellen, for instance, may be a tribute to the Welsh ancestry of the Tudors. That Shakespeare saw English history in this pattern cannot be doubted.

The first part of my argument is, that one of Shakespeare's main concerns in his last plays, whether deliberately taken up or fortuitously drifted into, was to develop the final phase of the tragic pattern, to add, as it were, his *Eumenides* to the already completed *Agamemnon* and *Choephoroe*, a process repeated by Milton when he supplemented *Paradise Lost* with *Samson Agonistes*.

But, as a preliminary, I must outline my conception of how the plays, immediately antecedent, come in the plan of Shakespeare's development. First, I accept (against E. K. Chambers) the usual opinion that *Timon* goes with *Lear*. 'The date of *Timon* is unknown,' says Dover Wilson, 'but unless it be the stillborn twin of *Lear* then we may give up talking about Shakespearian moods altogether.' The transitional plays between the full tragic period and the romances are *Antony and Cleopatra* and *Coriolanus*. Such A. C. Bradley took them to be; and his opinion is worth quoting. Referring to the final impression made by the two plays, he wrote:[1]

> This impression . . . can scarcely be called purely tragic; or, if we call it so, at least the feeling of reconciliation which

[1] *Shakespearean Tragedy* (2nd edition), p. 84.

mingles with the obviously tragic emotions is here exceptionally
well-marked. . . . The death of Cleopatra . . . is greeted by
the reader with admiration, even with exultation at the thought
that she has foiled Octavius; and these feelings are heightened
by the deaths of Charmian and Iras, heroically faithful to their
mistress. . . . In *Coriolanus* the feeling of reconciliation is even
stronger. . . . When he [Coriolanus] . . . gives way, although
we know he will lose his life, we care little for that: he has
saved his soul. Our relief, and our exultation in the power of
goodness, are so great that the actual catastrophe which follows
and mingles sadness with these feelings leaves them but little
diminished, and as we close the book we feel . . . more as we
do at the close of *Cymbeline* than as we do at the close of *Othello*.
. . . *Coriolanus* . . . marks the transition to the latest works, in
which the powers of repentance and forgiveness charm to rest
the tempest raised by error and guilt.

Now, in so far as Shakespeare was beginning in these two
plays to concern himself with the final, regenerative phase
of the tragic pattern, he was indeed beginning his process
of transition to the romances. But in neither play did he
portray the regenerative process at all completely or con-
vincingly. On the contrary, the hints of a regeneration
in the mind of Othello count for more than all the dying
ecstasies of Antony and Cleopatra or Coriolanus's yielding to his mother. The difference is this. Othello recognises his errors and transmutes them into his new state of
mind; Antony, Cleopatra, and Coriolanus abandon their
errors without transmuting them. Hence reconciliation
is not the word to apply to their states of mind. It is a
different thing to pass from A to B, and to fuse A and B
into an amalgam C. Antony does the first, Othello the
second. When St. Paul was converted he may have freed

himself from a kind of devil, but the fierce angel that was born in the conversion incorporated, among other things, that very devil from which he had broken free. That is the true reconciliation. The vacillations of Antony and his neglect of duty, the cunning and cruelty of Cleopatra, find no part in the creatures who are transfigured in death; they remain unassimilated, held in tension against the pair's expiring nobilities. The reason why *Antony and Cleopatra* is so baffling a play (and why the rhapsodies it provokes tend to be hysterical) is that the effort to see the two main characters simultaneously in two so different guises taxes our strength beyond our capacities. And yet that effort has to be made. Those who see Antony as the erring hero merely, and his final exaltation as ironic infatuation, are as partial in their judgment as those who think that his final heroics wash out his previous frailties. Both sets are part right, but each needs the other's truth to support it. In the same way, Coriolanus's submission to his mother is a single act, however impressive, which involves no regrouping, much less fusion and recasting of his previous qualities. His will has been overborne on that particular occasion. Now the latest plays aim at a complete regeneration; at a melting down of the old vessel and a recasting of it into something new. Thus Florizel and Perdita re-enact the marriage of Leontes and Hermione, but with better success.

There remains *Pericles*, and it may be asked why I am not considering it along with the other three romances. Although it is likely that the last three acts are mainly Shakespeare, there is no proof that he handled them seriously enough to justify our basing any elaborate theorising upon them. The scene of Marina's birth

(III. i.) does indeed touch the height of Shakespearean art, while the recognition of Pericles and Marina is very fine. The brothel scenes, though probably by Shakespeare, are not ultimately effective. The brothel is superbly described, but, seeing it primarily through Shakespeare's own sympathetic eyes, we can find little use for Marina in that setting. When Marina preaches at Boult and he replies:

> What would you have me do? go to the wars, would you? where a man may serve seven years for the loss of a leg and have not money enough in the end to buy him a wooden one,

it is Boult rather than Marina who catches our sympathy. We cannot indeed be at ease simultaneously with Marina and the other inmates of the brothel; and end by thinking her a prude, however strongly our reason insists that she would in point of fact and in all decency have been horrified at her plight and have behaved precisely as she is made to behave. If the brothel scenes are ineffective, except in isolation, the end, with the vision of Diana and the recognition of Thaisa in Ephesus, is scanty and ridiculous. Some of the play's versification, however, is important for our present purposes. In general, it quite lacks the fullness and complexity that mark most of the verse of the three last plays. On the other hand, there is heard now and then, and perhaps for the first time in Shakespeare, that simple yet strained, remote and magical note that sounds from time to time in the last plays and helps to give them their unique character. It enters into the Welsh scenes in *Cymbeline*, the statue scene in *The Winter's Tale*, and it may meet us at any moment in *The Tempest*. The last of these lines from

c

Pericles's farewell speech to Thaisa will serve to illustrate its early appearance in Shakespeare:

> A terrible childbed hast thou had, my dear;
> No light, no fire: the unfriendly elements
> Forgot thee utterly; nor have I time
> To give thee hallow'd to thy grave, but straight
> Must cast thee, scarcely coffin'd, in the ooze,
> Where, for a monument upon thy bones
> And aye-remaining lamps, the belching whale
> And humming water must o'erwhelm thy corpse,
> Lying with simple shells.

Still, it is wrong to extract from this novelty of music any more complex fact than that Shakespeare at the time of *Pericles* was being impelled along *some* new way of expression. The other features of the play are too haphazard and ill-organised to give any sure information whither that way was tending. It is for this reason that critics like Wilson Knight[1] and D. G. James,[2] who use *Pericles* as a base on which to erect their symbolic interpretations of Shakespeare's last plays, are taking the gravest risks. That Shakespeare handled the Pericles story may have been the merest accident. He may have approached it with the vaguest notion of what he might make of it. Nor is there the least reason to be sure that an incident occurring in *Pericles* bears the same significance as it does when repeated in a later play. Middleton Murry, to whose fitful capacity for penetrating common sense justice is not always done, may be quite right when he says:

[1] In *The Shakespearean Tempest.*
[2] In *Scepticism and Poetry.*

24

It is as certain as any conjecture of the kind can be that *Pericles* struck Shakespeare, while he worked upon it, as a thing full of potentialities.

As a seminal play, rich in undeveloped possibilities, we may heed it, but not as something embodying any fully formed experience in Shakespeare's mind.

Setting aside *Pericles*, therefore, let me return for a moment to *Antony and Cleopatra*. I said that Antony's frailties were not assimilated into his magnificences. And indeed his magnificences are but a part of his old self, intensified. Part of his world collapses; the other part, his love for Cleopatra, remains. Unencumbered by imperial duties, but not in any way springing from the wreck of them, it touches a sublime consummation in the fourth act of the play.

But in the last three plays the old order is destroyed as thoroughly as in the main group of tragedies, and it is this destruction that altogether separates them from the realm of comedy in general and from Shakespeare's own earlier comedies in particular. In comedy the vagaries of the individual are judged by the permanent standards of society, and are made in the end to conform to those standards. In some of Shakespeare's comedies—in *Much Ado*, for instance—there is the risk of destruction. Beatrice, when she blazes out into her fierce appeal to Benedick to 'kill Claudio' for his treatment of Hero, is potentially a tragic figure, but actually Dogberry and his men save the situation. And in the end the villain is thwarted, Benedick and Beatrice are good-humouredly mocked for their charming eccentricities, and the audience finds itself in the same old world, only aired, exercised, and regaled with marriage-bells.

Examining the bare plots rather than the total impression of the last three plays, we find in each the same general scheme of prosperity, destruction, and re-creation. The main character is a King. At the beginning he is in prosperity. He then does an evil or misguided deed. Great suffering follows, but during this suffering or at its height the seeds of something new to issue from it are germinating, usually in secret. In the end this new element assimilates and transforms the old evil. The King overcomes his evil instincts, joins himself to the new order by an act of forgiveness or repentance; and the play issues into a fairer prosperity than had first existed.

ii. Cymbeline

The beginning of *Cymbeline* and the reason why the play bears that name are hidden from us till half-way through, when Belarius tells us:

> O Cymbeline! heaven and my conscience knows
> Thou didst unjustly banish me: whereon,
> At three and two years old, I stole these babes;
> Thinking to bar thee of succession, as
> Thou reft'st me of my lands.

Cymbeline begins in prosperity, but he commits the error of suspecting the innocent and trusting the vicious. He banishes Belarius and takes a bad woman for his second wife. The immediate consequence is that he loses his two sons. The later consequence is that he loses his remaining child, Imogen, whom he had hoped to marry to his step-son. At the same time a new life is being created through these same lost children. The Welsh hills are, as it were, the womb in which the new life is growing to a birth. It is not for mere romantic variety alone that Imogen, persecuted in her parents' home, finds refuge with her brothers. She, too, is a part of the new life. Meanwhile, Cymbeline goes to war with the Romans. The rottenness of what he and his then state of mind stand for is imaged in the disgraceful panic into which his army falls, and his own capture. From this plight he and his army are rescued by his lost sons, now mature and broken free from their mountain-hold, by the old man who stole and educated them, and by another character, Posthumus, who has by now renounced his sins and become regenerate in humiliation. This sudden assertion of the new element restores the fortunes of Cymbeline and puts the whole ordering of events in his hands. Prone at first to vengeance on his Roman captives, he ends by forswearing his old evil self and accepts the new order by forgiving Belarius and sparing his captives. In anticipatory reward his bad queen had conveniently died, and in present reward his children are restored to him. The end is even more prosperous than the beginning.

Bearing in mind the very close connection of the last three plays, and arguing back a little from the last two to *Cymbeline*, we cannot doubt that the above account truly represents part of that play's intention. Reading the play without paying special heed to the plot, we have to confess that this intention is very feebly expressed. Half a dozen other things emerge more vividly. The tragic events (for which Cymbeline's original error is ultimately responsible) are curiously apt to end in insignificance, while the new existence into which the tragic action issues is, as any recognisable and convincing way of life, a pallid and bloodless affair. By making an intellectual abstract of the plot we may convince ourselves that Cymbeline is regenerate at the end of the play; but from reading the play we can only say that he fails to stir our imagination and that his regeneration is a thing quite dead.

A good example of tragedy petering out is Posthumus's soliloquy after Iachimo has proved to him Imogen's guilt (Act ii. v.). Iachimo describes his supposed seduction of Imogen and plays his victim with consummate skill and coolness. There is perfection of economy and finish: and all is ready for a genuine flow of fear and pity for Posthumus in his plight. But his soliloquy lets us down. For a line or two he may hover on the brink of deep feeling and hint at a mental turmoil resembling Troilus's when confronted with Cressida's infidelity:

> O, vengeance, vengeance!
> Me of my lawful pleasure she restrain'd
> And pray'd me oft forbearance; did it with
> A pudency so rosy the sweet view on't
> Might well have warm'd Old Saturn; that I thought her
> As chaste as unsunn'd snow. O, all the devils!
> This yellow Iachimo, in an hour,—was't not?—
> Or less,—at first?—perchance he spoke not, but,
> Like a full-acorn'd boar, a German one,
> Cried 'O!' and mounted.

But the speech issues into a conventional cynicism like that of Donne's satires, and into the surprising frigidity (suggesting that Shakespeare was deliberately satirising the satirists) of declaring that he will *write* against women:

28

>   Could I find out
> The woman's part in me!   For there's no motion
> That tends to vice in man, but I affirm
> It is the woman's part: be it lying, note it,
> The woman's; flattering, hers; deceiving, hers;
> Lust and rank thoughts, hers, hers; revenges, hers;
> Ambitions, covetings, change of pride, disdain,
> Nice longing, slanders, mutability,
> All faults that may be named, nay, that hell knows,
> Why, hers, in part or all; but rather, all;
> For even to vice
> They are not constant, but are changing still
> One vice, but of a minute old, for one
> Not half so old as that.   I'll write against them,
> Detest them, curse them: yet 'tis greater skill
> In a true hate, to pray they have their will:
> The very devils cannot plague them better.

This is delightful and rousing rhetoric, but quite remote from tragic feeling, and the worst possible preparation for Posthumus's solemn penitence when he reappears in Act v.

But if this scene lets us down, Imogen does so far worse. Far worse, because she is the chief character, the only one on whom attention is bent throughout the course of the play and who had any chance of giving unity to the miscellany of events that are represented in it. Moreover, it is she who bears the heaviest burden of misfortune and whom one could expect to express the chief share of tragic emotion, and she has a unique importance as a bridge between the old world of the court and the new world in the Welsh hills.

Though Imogen can no longer pass, as she did in the nineteenth century, for the dream-woman of wedded perfection, the chaste, the warm-hearted, the self-sacrificing, she by no means fits E. K. Chambers's description of her as a puppet:

> The puppet Imogen, set between the puppet Cloten and the puppet Posthumus, may pass for perfection, so long as the danger of comparison with the flesh and blood of Cleopatra or even of a Cressida is scrupulously avoided.

But Cleopatra is superfluous to this dangerous comparison, for Imogen provides it within herself. When she unhesitatingly accepts Iachimo's explanation of why he insulted the character of her husband, namely, that he was testing her fidelity, she is indeed a puppet. But set beside this acceptance the scene, coming not long after, where she rebuffs Cloten; and she shows up a complete human being. The scene (beginning II. iii. 91) is a brilliantly realistic picture of a good-humoured but high-spirited girl anxious to behave as well as she can to the disgusting Cloten, but in the end roused to cruel resentment and bitterness of tongue. Here are three stages in her feelings. First, cool and courteous deprecation in answer to his first greeting:

> Good morrow, sir. You lay out too much pains
> For purchasing but trouble: the thanks I give
> Is telling you that I am poor of thanks
> And scarce can spare them.

Then, a little later, warmer but still courteous denial, with a touch of sarcasm she has not been able to control:

> But that you shall not say I yield, being silent,
> I would not speak. I pray you, spare me: 'faith,
> I shall unfold equal discourtesy
> To your best kindness: one of your great knowing
> Should learn, being taught, forbearance.

And finally, when Cloten taunts Posthumus, she answers furiously:

> He never can meet more mischance than come
> To be but named of thee.   His meanest garment,
> That ever hath but clipp'd his body, is dearer
> In my respect than all the hairs above thee,
> Were they all made such men.   How now, Pisanio!

And when Pisanio enters, her words to him express wonderfully her complicated feelings: fury just on the wane, shame at hàving lost her temper, assurance that she yet had every reason to lose it:

> I am sprited with a fool,
> Frighted, and anger'd worse: go bid my woman
> Search for a jewel that too casually
> Hath left mine arm.

It is a scene of this sort that makes it the more disappointing when she turns into a purely conventional figure. Judged by the standards of her most lifelike self, her cheerful readiness (so soon after her tragic appeals for death at Pisanio's hand) to dress up as a boy is nothing short of frivolous.   Moreover, there is a deep discrepancy between her occasional warm-hearted humanity and her cold and conventional chastity:

> Me of my lawful pleasure she restrain'd
> And pray'd me oft forbearance,

said Posthumus. And while her husband is absent, she insists on waking at midnight like a nun. She 'lies in watch' and thinks of him and 'weeps 'twixt clock and clock.' The truth is that Imogen is at times a human being, at times a Griselda of the medieval imagination.

Nor is it any use trying to regard her as primarily the one or the other, and her aberrations from her primary rôle as the exceptions. Once she has had the boy's disguise imposed on her, she loses all possibility of dignity as a human being; and in her part as Griselda she is too weakly portrayed to be significant as a symbol. We may enjoy her isolated splendours, her outbursts of true human feeling, or the lovely poetry that passes her lips, but as a great character we must simply give her up.

Why Shakespeare should have troubled himself with her as much as he did and yet reduced her to ineffectiveness is a question to which it is easy enough to retort with half a dozen answers, all equally incapable of proof. On the other hand, I doubt the possibility of truth in any retort that does not insist on some unusual uncertainty in Shakespeare's mind. Though I agree with Granville-Barker that the technical artlessnesses of the play are 'sophisticated' and not 'native,' and that part of Shakespeare's aim in the play was a very self-conscious prettiness, these qualities do not really account for the strenuousness that went to create Imogen and to write certain great scenes, a strenuousness whose existence is not annulled because it, in the end, achieves so little. It may be that with the writing of *Pericles* Shakespeare concluded that romantic material was in some way suited to expressing that phase of the tragic pattern to which he was now drawn. But he is as yet uncertain how to manipulate, in what proportions to blend the preponderatingly human treatment of character he used in the tragedies with the more symbolic treatment found generally in romance.

That he had set himself this problem is likely, from a certain resemblance which *Cymbeline* presents to parts of

32

Arcadia. For the most cogent reason for Shakespeare's turning from Plutarch to romance I must refer the reader to a later page, but *Arcadia*, in its main plot, supplies that total development from prosperity to an upsetting of the balance, to suffering, and to a final more excellent state, which Shakespeare seems now drawn to deal with. And it should be remembered that not long before, Shakespeare had taken the sub-plot of *Lear* from *Arcadia*. Common to *Cymbeline* and *Arcadia* is the blend of classical and medieval, of political events and romantic setting. And both authors, for all the wild improbabilities or minor inconsistencies they allow, keep a firm intellectual grip on the main complexities of their plots. Cymbeline, with his irresolute character and his weak dealing with his wife, is not unlike Basilius, while the relations of the Queen, Cloten, and Imogen are nearly the same as those of Cecropia, Amphialus, and Philoclea. Both queens are wicked, and both seek to marry their sons to princesses whom they hold in captivity and use spitefully. But Sidney, granted his inferior powers, makes a better job of the very same problem that faced Shakespeare, the problem of blending the human and the symbolic treatment of character. Beginning from the side of romance, he gives Philoclea little human warmth; she is a pattern of sweet and reserved girlhood. Later, when she is captured and subjected to Amphialus's courtship and to Cecropia's varied attempts to break her spirit, she quickens into a faint kind of life; as in this passage describing Cecropia's first attempt to gain her for Amphialus:

'Your fortune,' said Cecropia, 'if she could see to attire herself, she would put on her best raiments. For I see, and I see it with grief, you misconstrue everything that only for your sake is attempted. . . . And truly I had a thing to say unto you, but it is no matter; since I find you are so obstinately melancholy, I will spare my pains and hold my peace'—and so stayed indeed, thinking Philoclea would have had a female inquisitiveness of the matter. But she, who rather wished to unknow what she knew than to burden her heart with more hopeless knowledge, only desired her to have pity of her, and if indeed she did mean her no hurt, then to grant her liberty; for else the very grief and fear would prove her unappointed executioners.

Her sister, Pamela, develops in the same way. She begins as a bright but inhuman pattern of high-spirited virginity. Later, in captivity, when she suffers mental and physical torture, she takes on some likeness to a human being. Further, the contrast between the two sisters, not very significant in the earlier part of the book, shows up with some effect when they are in captivity. Now by becoming human Philoclea and Pamela acquire a power which supplements but does not extinguish their previous (and quite successful) symbolic significance. With Imogen Shakespeare did the opposite. New to the technique of the romance and accustomed to that of the drama, he began by making an, on the whole, human and sentient character, with the result that any subsequent attempt to make her a symbol appears chilly and bloodless after the initial warmth.

That in this adjustment of tragic and romantic features, of realistic and symbolic character, Shakespeare was feeling his way in *Cymbeline*, was trying different methods, seems likely, because in Imogen's brothers we have two characters fashioned not like her but like Sidney's Philoclea and Pamela. They meet us first as symbols of the kingly nature blooming in wild surroundings. And they are quite successful as far as they go, which is not very far. When Shakespeare adds a certain measure of humanity to them, as he does, we are grateful but do not forget their prime symbolic significance. They are, indeed, very skilfully differentiated. Guiderius, the elder, the future King, is quick, practical, and not too imaginative, as Shakespeare thought a ruler should be: like Theseus and Henry V. He sums up Cloten's character with quick shrewdness and disposes of him and his head with summary coolness. Arviragus is imaginative, and some of the most poetical passages in the play are put in his mouth. Their different characters come out best when, after Arviragus has let his imagination play on the way he will deck the grave of the still unburied Fidele (the passage Collins turned into his *Dirge in Cymbeline*), Polydore brings him back to business with

> Prithee, have done;
> And do not play in wench-like words with that
> Which is so serious. Let us bury him,
> And not protract with admiration what
> Is now due debt. To the grave!

It is interesting that though Shakespeare made a great failure of Imogen and a minor success of her brothers, he did not use his successful method when he came to re-handle their functions in *The Winter's Tale*. He repeats the method he used for Imogen, beginning with realism and continuing with symbol. But he solves his problem by splitting her into two persons: Hermione, the real woman; Perdita, though so much else, the symbol. In a new country, after a lapse of years, and through a second character, we can easily accept that change of method which in a single character asked too much of our credulity.

Shakespeare's difficulties in *Cymbeline* may be better understood by a comparison with D. H. Lawrence's when he was in process of changing his methods from those of *Sons and Lovers* at one end to those of *The Plumed Serpent* at the other. In *Sons and Lovers* the characters are realistic, in *The Plumed Serpent* symbolical. Lawrence, of course, differed from Shakespeare in having a more prophetic and apocalyptic mind, which naturally inclined to make his characters embody spiritual forces rather than give back the variegation of real life. Hence he passed from realism to symbol much earlier in his literary career. But, granted this difference, he shows the same process and the same confusion during the period of transition. *Women in Love* is confused much after the manner of *Cymbeline*. Here Ursula and Gudrun, Birkin and Gerald Critch begin their existence as human beings in the world of men, owning a complexity that ties them with some force to their kin. At the end of the book they have become, in the main, symbols of large but isolated human impulses (Gerald, for example, of the will to power) set in an Alpine setting which is at once realistic (for Lawrence never forfeited his genius for being close to natural things) and symbolic of a strenuous and exalted realm of mental activity. Even in a small detail the change can be seen. Gudrun in the first chapter is wearing emerald-green stockings, which are very appropriate to the 'arty' young woman who owns them. And we hear something from time to time about Gudrun's stockings. Near the end of the book the sisters talk over the issue of their Tyrolese holiday. It is the culminating scene; and to get it going, Lawrence introduces Gudrun's stockings. The conversation in which they figure is realistic, yet the stockings have ceased to be a mere appropriate appendage and become symbols of Gudrun's inner self:

> Gudrun came to Ursula's bedroom with three pairs of the coloured stockings for which she was notorious, and she threw them on the bed. But these were thick silk stockings, vermilion, cornflower blue, and grey, bought in Paris. The grey ones were knitted, seamless and heavy. Ursula was in raptures. She knew Gudrun must be feeling *very* loving, to give away such treasures.
>
> 'I can't take them from you, Prune,' she cried. 'I can't possibly deprive you of them—the jewels.'
>
> 'Aren't they jewels!' cried Gudrun, eyeing her gifts with an envious eye. 'Aren't they real lambs!'
>
> 'Yes, you *must* keep them,' said Ursula.
>
> 'I don't *want* them, I've got three more pairs. I *want* you to keep them—I want you to have them. They're yours, there——'
>
> And with trembling, excited hands she put the coveted stockings under Ursula's pillow.
>
> 'One gets the greatest joy of all out of really lovely stockings,' said Ursula.
>
> 'One does,' replied Gudrun; 'the greatest joy of all.'

And because the stockings have been transformed, we can the better accept the sisters' symbolic functions: Gudrun standing for the self-sufficiency of earthly love, Ursula for a state beyond the earthly in which love is included:

> Gudrun reflected for a few moments. Then a smile of ridicule, almost of contempt, came over her face.

37

'And what will happen when you find yourself in space?' she cried in derision. 'After all, the great ideas of the world are the same there. You above everybody can't get away from the fact that love, for instance, is the supreme thing, in space as well as on earth.'

'No,' said Ursula, 'it isn't. Love is too human and little. I believe in something inhuman, of which love is only a little part. I believe what we must fulfil comes out of the unknown to us, and it is something infinitely more than love. It isn't so merely human.'

Gudrun looked at Ursula with steady, balancing eyes. She admired and despised her sister so much, both! Then, suddenly she averted her face, saying coldly, uglily:

'Well, I've got no further than love, yet.'

Over Ursula's mind flashed the thought: 'Because you never *have* loved, you can't get beyond it.'

In its context the scene is impressive, and we do not demur at the sisters having become mouthpieces for ideas that fought in Lawrence's brain rather than recognisable women. But in *Women in Love* Lawrence achieves his symbolic method only fitfully and through a wearisome expense of effort. As in *Cymbeline*, there are fine and moving human episodes (for instance, Diana's death by drowning in the lake, old Mr. Critch's dying agonies), belonging to the world of men, yet they lead nowhere because their author created them in a manner from which he was even then escaping and which he must unconsciously have distrusted. The bulk of *Women in Love*, for all its wealth of fine incident, is dull and insignificant. Just so *Cymbeline's* significance is small compared with the fine things it contains, though Shakespeare's brilliant and sophisticated manipulation of

38

incident (merely as incident with the immediate appeal of novelty) makes the play lively enough to witness.

When Lawrence settles to his symbolic treatment of character he is much less sure than the Shakespeare of *The Winter's Tale* and *The Tempest* in the art of enlivening symbol with realism.   Yet he has his successes in this art, and these may be compared with Sidney's treatment of Philoclea and Pamela, and Shakespeare's of Guiderius and Arviragus, as described above.   Kate, the heroine of *The Plumed Serpent*, is not a realistic human being but a symbol of what remnant of healthy life-instinct Lawrence still detects under the oppression of western civilisation. This symbol is brought at the beginning against the terrible account of the bull-fight, itself symbolic indeed of the utmost degradation that western civilisation has fallen into, but acutely realistic.   And the blend of method is entirely successful.   At the very end of the book Lawrence does the same with the sureness of a master. The plot of the book consists of the woman's gradually casting off her western way of life and taking on the new way inherited from the old Mexican religion.   Just after she has married Cipriano, and yet before she has made the final surrender, she longs to break away and go home.   And this longing is conveyed through the slight realistic touch of showing London busy with Christmas preparations:

'How awful, Christmas with hibiscus and poinsettia!   It makes me long to see mistletoe among the oranges, in a fruiterer's shop in Hampstead!'

'Why that?' laughed Teresa.

'Oh!' Kate sighed petulantly.   'To get back to simple life. To see the 'buses rolling on the mud in Piccadilly, on Christmas

Eve, and the wet pavements crowded with people under the brilliant shops.'

The art that set this realism beside the remote and the symbolic is not unlike the one that passed suddenly from the 'golden lads and girls' to the 'chimney-sweepers.'

To return from this digression to the tragic pattern in *Cymbeline*. It looks as if Shakespeare knew that what he wanted to express could be expressed through the cycle of prosperity, destruction, and renewed prosperity, and that the complex material of the prose romance was in some ways congenial to his needs. Yet he is unable to adjust his methods to the new wealth of content; with the result that his main concern becomes blurred and remote, and the details become more emphatic than the end it was their business to forward.

iii. The Winter's Tale

In *The Winter's Tale* Shakespeare omitted all the irrelevancies that had clotted *Cymbeline*, and presented the whole tragic pattern, from prosperity to destruction, regeneration, and still fairer prosperity, in full view of the audience. This is a bold, frontal attack on the problem, necessitating the complete disregard of the unity of time; but it succeeded, as far as success was possible within the bounds of a single play. One difference in plot from *Cymbeline* is, that there is little overlap between the old and the new life. In Guiderius and Arviragus the new life had been incubating for years while the old life held sway in Cymbeline and his court. But Perdita, chief symbol of the new life, has not lived many hours before Leontes begins his own conversion.

Unlike *Cymbeline*, the first half of the play is seriously tragic and could have included Hermione's death, like Greene's *Pandosto*. Leontes's obsession of jealousy is terrifying in its intensity. It reminds us not of other Shakespearean tragic errors, but rather of the god-sent lunacies of Greek drama, the lunacies of Ajax and Heracles. It is as scantily motivated as these, and we should refrain from demanding any motive. Indeed, it is as much a surprise to the characters in the play as it is to the reader, and its nature is that of an earthquake or the loss of the 'Titanic' rather than of rational human psychology. And equally terrifying is Leontes's cry, when, after defying the oracle, he hears of his son's death:

> Apollo's angry; and the heavens themselves
> Do strike at my injustice.

Hermione's character is far more firmly based on probability than Imogen's. There is nothing strained or hectic about her love for her husband: it is rooted in habit. And when at her trial, addressing Leontes, she says:

> To me can life be no commodity;
> The crown and comfort of my life, your favour,
> I do give lost; for I do feel it gone,
> But know not how it went,

we accept the statement as sober truth. While for distilled pathos no poet, not even Euripides, has excelled

her final soliloquy, when she realises Leontes's fixed
hostility:

> The Emperor of Russia was my father:
> O that he were alive, and here beholding
> His daughter's trial! that he did but see
> The flatness of my misery, yet with eyes
> Of pity, not revenge!

In sum, the first half of the play renders worthily, in the
main through a realistic method, the destructive portion
of the tragic pattern.

Now, although Leontes and Hermione live on to give
continuity to the play and although the main tragic
pattern is worked out nominally in Leontes, the royal
person, it is not they in their reconciliation who most
create the feeling of rebirth. At the best they mend the
broken vessel of their fortunes with glue or seccotine;
and our imaginations are not in the least stirred by any
future life that we can conceive the pair enjoying together.
Were the pattern of destruction and regeneration the sole
motive of the play, the statue scene would have little
point and be, as Middleton Murry calls it, a theatrical
trick. But the continued existence of Leontes and Hermione is a matter of subordinate expediency; and it is
Florizel and Perdita and the countryside where they meet
which make the new life.

And here I must plead as earnestly as I can for allowing
more than the usual virtue and weight to the fourth act of
The Winter's Tale. There are several reasons why it has
been taken too lightly. It has been far too much the
property of vague young women doing eurhythmics at
Speech Days or on vicarage lawns; and, when it is acted
professionally, the part of Perdita is usually taken by

some pretty little fool or pert suburban charmer. Also, it is usually thought that joy and virtue are inferior as poetic themes to suffering and vice; or that the earthly paradise taxed the resources of Dante less than Ugolino's tower. It would seem that the truth is the other way round, because convincing pictures of joy and virtue are extremely rare, while those of suffering and vice are comparatively common. Shelley succeeds in describing the sufferings of Prometheus; the earthly bliss brought on by them is, except in patches, a shoddy affair in comparison. Shakespeare never did anything finer, more serious, more evocative of his full powers, than his picture of an earthly paradise painted in the form of the English countryside. The old problem of adjusting realism and symbol is so well solved that we are quite unconscious of it. The country life is given the fullest force of actuality, as when the old shepherd describes his wife's hospitality at the shearing feast:

> Fie, daughter! when my old wife lived, upon
> This day she was both pantler, butler, cook,
> Both dame and servant; welcomed all, served all:
> Would sing her song and dance her turn; now here,
> At upper end o' the table, now i' the middle;
> On his shoulder, and his; her face o' fire
> With labour and the thing she took to quench it,
> She would to each one sip.

Yet the whole country setting stands out as the cleanest and most elegant symbol of the new life into which the old horrors are to be transmuted.

It is the same with the characters. Shakespeare blends the realistic and the symbolic with the surest touch.

Florizel, who is kept a rather flat character the more to show up Perdita, one would call a type rather than a symbol; but for the play's purposes he is an efficient type of chivalry and generosity. He will not let down Perdita, but defies his father at the risk of losing a kingdom:

> I am not sorry, not afeard; delay'd
> But nothing altered: what I was, I am;
> More straining on for plucking back, not following
> My leash unwillingly.

Perdita, on the other hand, is one of Shakespeare's richest characters; at once a symbol and a human being. She is the play's main symbol of the powers of creation. And rightly, because, as Leontes was the sole agent of destruction, so it is fitting, ironically fitting, that the one of his kin whom he had thrown out as bastard should embody the contrary process. Not that Leontes, as a character, is the contrary to Perdita. *His* obsession is not a part of his character but an accretion. Her true contrary is Iago. It is curious that Iago should ever have been thought motiveless. The desire to destroy is a very simple derivative from the power-instinct, the instinct which in its evil form goes by the name of the first of the deadly sins, Pride. It was by that sin that the angels fell, and at the end of *Othello* Iago is explicitly equated with the Devil. Shakespeare embodied all his horror of this type of original sin in Iago. He was equally aware of original virtue, and he pictured it, in Perdita, blossoming spontaneously in the simplest of country settings. There is little direct reference to her instincts to create; but they are implied by her sympathy with nature's lavishness in producing flowers, followed by her own simple and unashamed confession of wholesome sensuality. The whole passage, so often confined to mere idyllic description, must be quoted in hopes that the reader will allow the profounder significance I claim for it. Perdita is talking to her guests, to Polixenes, Camillo, and Florizel in particular:

Per.   Here's flowers for you;
        Hot lavender, mints, savory, marjoram;
        The marigold, that goes to bed wi' the sun
        And with him rises weeping: these are flowers
        Of middle summer, and I think they are given
        To men of middle age. You're very welcome.
Cam. I should leave grazing, were I of your flock,
        And only live by gazing.
Per.   Out, alas!
        You'ld be so lean, that blasts of January
        Would blow you through and through. Now, my fair'st
            friend,
        I would I had some flowers o' the spring that might
        Become your time of day; and yours, and yours,
        That wear upon your virgin branches yet
        Your maidenheads growing: O Proserpina,
        For the flowers now, that frighted thou let'st fall
        From Dis's wagon! daffodils,
        That come before the swallow dares, and take
        The winds of March with beauty; violets dim,
        But sweeter than the lids of Juno's eyes
        Or Cytherea's breath; pale primroses,
        That die unmarried, ere they can behold
        Bright Phoebus in his strength—a malady
        Most incident to maids; bold oxlips and
        The crown imperial; lilies of all kinds,

45

> The flower-de-luce being one!   O, these I lack,
> To make you garlands of, and my sweet friend,
> To strew him o'er and o'er.
>
> *Flo.*   What, like a corse?
> *Per.* No, like a bank for love to lie and play on;
>   Not like a corse; or if, not to be buried,
>   But quick and in mine arms.

The great significance of Perdita's lines lies partly in the verse, which (especially at the close) is leisurely, full, assured, matured, suggestive of fruition, and acutely contrasted to the tortured, arid, and barren ravings of Leontes, and which reinforces that kinship with nature and healthy sensuality mentioned above.   But it lies also in the references to the classical Pantheon.   The gods of Greece and Rome occur very frequently in the last plays of Shakespeare and are certainly more than mere embroidery.   Apollo is the dominant god in *The Winter's Tale*, and his appearance in Perdita's speech is meant to quicken the reader to apprehend some unusual significance.   He appears as the bridegroom, whom the pale primroses never know, but who visits the other flowers. Not to take the fertility symbolism as intended would be a perverse act of caution.   Perdita should be associated with them, as symbol both of the creative powers of nature, physical fertility, and of healing and re-creation of the mind.   She is like Milton's youthful Ceres,

> Yet virgin of Proserpina from Jove,

or his Eve, mistress of the flowers of Paradise.

The health of Perdita's natural instincts not only helps her symbolic force; it helps to make her a realistic character.   Other parts of her character are a deep-seated strength and ruthless common sense. She argues coolly with Polixenes about art and nature, and is not frightened by his later fulminations, saying when he has gone:

> I was not much afeard; for once or twice
> I was about to speak and tell him plainly,
> The selfsame sun that shines upon his court
> Hides not his visage from our cottage but
> Looks on alike.

At the same time she shows that she has been all the time quite without illusions about the danger she runs in loving Florizel, the Prince, and when the shock comes with the discovery of their plighted love she is prepared without fuss to accept her fate. Turning to Florizel, she goes on:

> Will't please you, sir, be gone?
> I told you what would come of this: beseech you,
> Of your own state take care: this dream of mine—
> Being now awake, I'll queen it no inch farther,
> But milk my ewes and weep.

It is through Perdita's magnificence that we accept as valuable the new life into which the play is made to issue. The disadvantage of centring the creative processes in her and Florizel is structural. There is a break in continuity; for though Perdita is born in the first half of the play, as characters the pair are new to the last half. And we have juxtaposition, not organic growth. There is no Orestes to lead from the *Choephoroe* to the *Eumenides*. On the other hand, I find this juxtaposition easy enough to accept; and it is mitigated by Perdita's parentage. She is Hermione's true daughter and prolongs in herself those regenerative processes which in her mother have suffered a temporary eclipse.

The common praise of Autolycus as a character is well justified. It is likely that he is organic to the whole country scene, and that it would collapse into an over-sweetness of sentiment without him. Though he comes and goes with the aloofness of an elf among humans, he is united with the other characters in his admirable adjust-ment to the country life. His delinquencies, like the pastoral realism, keep the earthly paradise sufficiently earthly without disturbing the paradisiac state; for they are anti-toxic rather than toxic, harmless to vigorous health, and an efficient prophylactic against the lotus-fruit which, as a drug, has so greatly impaired the health of most earthly paradises.

iv. The Tempest

It is a common notion that *Cymbeline* and *The Winter's Tale* are experiments leading to the final success of *The Tempest*. I think it quite untrue of *The Winter's Tale*, which, in some ways though not in others, deals with the tragic pattern more adequately than the later play. Cer-tainly it deals with the destructive portion more directly and fully. On the other hand, *The Tempest*, by keeping this destructive portion largely in the background and dealing mainly with regeneration, avoids the juxtaposition of the two themes, which some people (of whom I am not one) find awkward in *The Winter's Tale*. The simple truth is, that if you cram a trilogy into a single play something has to be sacrificed. Shakespeare chose to make a different sacrifice in each of his two successful renderings of the complete tragic pattern: unity in *The*

Winter's Tale, present rendering of the destructive part of the tragic pattern in *The Tempest*.

Many readers, drugged by the heavy enchantments of Prospero's island, may demur at my admitting the tragic element to the play at all. I can cite in support one of the latest studies of the play, Dover Wilson's [1] (although I differ somewhat in the way I think the tragic element is worked out). Of the storm scene he writes:

> It is as if Shakespeare had packed his whole tragic vision of life into one brief scene before bestowing his new vision upon us.

But one has only to look at the total plot to see that in its main lines it closely follows those of *Cymbeline* and *The Winter's Tale*, and that tragedy is an organic part of it. Prospero, when one first hears of him, was the ruler of an independent state and beloved of his subjects. But all is not well, because the King of Naples is his enemy. Like Basilius in Sidney's *Arcadia*, he commits the error of not attending carefully enough to affairs of state. The reason for this error, his Aristotelian ἁμαρτία, is his love of study. He hands over the government to his brother Antonio, who proceeds to call in the King of Naples to turn Prospero out of his kingdom. Fearing the people, Antonio refrains from murdering Prospero and his infant daughter, but sets them adrift in a boat. Now, except for this last item, the plot is entirely typical of Elizabethan revenge tragedy. Allow Prospero to be put to death, give him a son instead of a daughter to live and to avenge him, and your tragic plot is complete. Such are the

---

[1] *The Meaning of the Tempest*, the Robert Spence Watson Memorial Lecture for 1936, delivered before the Literary and Philosophical Society of Newcastle-upon-Tyne, on October 5th, 1936.

affinities of the actual plot of *The Tempest*. And in the abstract it is more typically tragic in the fashion of its age than *The Winter's Tale*, with its debt to the Greek romances.

In handling the theme of regeneration, Shakespeare in one way alters his method. Although a royal person had previously been the protagonist, it had been only in name. Cymbeline had indeed resembled Prospero in having his enemies at his mercy and in forgiving them, but he owed his power not to himself, but to fortune and the efforts of others. As for Leontes, he has little to do with his own regeneration; for it would be perverse to make too much of his generosity in sheltering Florizel and Perdita from the anger of Polixenes. But Prospero is the agent of his own regeneration, the parent and tutor of Miranda; and through her and through his own works he changes the minds of his enemies. It was by this centring of motives in Prospero as well as by subordinating the theme of destruction that Shakespeare gave *The Tempest* its unified structure.

In executing his work, Shakespeare chose a method new to himself but repeated by Milton in *Samson Agonistes*. He began his action at a point in the story so late that the story was virtually over; and he included the total story either by narrating the past or by re-enacting samples of it: a complete reaction from the method of frontal attack used in *The Winter's Tale*.

For the re-enactment of tragedy it is possible to think with Dover Wilson that the storm scene does this. But it does nothing to re-enact the specific tragic plot in the play, the fall of Prospero; and one of its aims is to sketch (as it does with incomparable swiftness) the characters of the ship's company. The true re-enactment is in the long first scene of the second act where Antonio, in persuading Sebastian to murder Alonso, personates his own earlier action in plotting against Prospero, thus drawing it out of the past and placing it before us in the present. This long scene, showing the shipwrecked King and courtiers and the conspiracy, has not had sufficient praise nor sufficient attention. Antonio's transformation from the cynical and lazy badgerer of Gonzalo's loquacity to the brilliantly swift and unscrupulous man of action is a thrilling affair. Just so Iago awakes from his churlish 'honesty' to his brilliant machinations. Antonio is indeed one of Shakespeare's major villains:

Ant.   Will you grant with me
    That Ferdinand is drown'd?
Seb.   He's gone.
Ant.   Then, tell me,
    Who's the next heir to Naples?
Seb.   Claribel.
Ant. She that is queen of Tunis; she that dwells
    Ten leagues beyond man's life; she that from Naples
    Can have no note, unless the sun were post—
    The man i' the moon's too slow—till new-born chins
    Be rough and razorable; she that from whom
    We all were sea-swallow'd, though some cast again,
    And by that destiny, to perform an act
    Whereof what's past is prologue, what to come,
    In yours and my discharge.
Seb.   What stuff is this! how say you?
    'Tis true my brother's daughter's queen of Tunis;
    So is she heir of Naples; 'twixt which regions
    There is some space.

Ant.   A space whose every cubit
    Seems to cry out, 'How shall that Claribel
    Measure us back to Naples? Keep in Tunis,
    And let Sebastian wake.' Say this were death
    That now hath seized them ; why, they were no worse
    Than now they are. There be that can rule Naples
    As well as he that sleeps; lords that can prate
    As amply and unnecessarily
    As this Gonzalo; I myself could make
    A chough of as deep chat. O, that you bore
    The mind that I do! What a sleep were this
    For your advancement! Do you understand me?

We should do wrong to take the conspiracy very seriously
in itself. We know Prospero's power, and when Ariel
enters and wakes the intended victims we have no fears
for their future safety. But all the more weight should
the scene assume as recalling the past.

Dover Wilson [1] greatly contributes to a right understanding of the play by stressing the first lines of the
fifth act, when Prospero declares to Ariel that he will
pardon his enemies, now quite at his mercy:

Ari.   Your charm so strongly works 'em
    That if you now beheld them, your affections
    Would become tender.
Pros.   Dost thou think so, spirit?
Ari. Mine would, sir, were I human.
Pros.   And mine shall.
    Hast thou, which art but air, a touch, a feeling
    Of their afflictions, and shall not myself,
    One of their kind, that relish all as sharply,
    Passion as they, be kindlier moved than thou art?

[1] *Op. cit.*, pp. 14-18.

> Though with their high wrongs I am struck to the quick,
> Yet with my nobler reason 'gainst my fury
> Do I take part: the rarer action is
> In virtue than in vengeance: they being penitent,
> The sole drift of my purpose doth extend
> Not a frown further.

But when Dover Wilson would have this to represent Prospero's sudden conversion from a previously intended vengeance, I cannot follow him. It is true that Prospero shows a certain haste of temper up to that point of the play, and that he punishes Caliban and the two other conspirators against his life with some asperity; but his comments on them, after his supposed conversion, have for me the old ring:

> Mark but the badges of these men, my lords,
> Then say if they be true. This mis-shapen knave,
> His mother was a witch, and one so strong
> That could control the moon, make flows and ebbs,
> And deal in her command without her power.
> These three have robb'd me; and this demi-devil—
> For he's a bastard one—had plotted with them
> To take my life. Two of these fellows you
> Must know and own; this thing of darkness I
> Acknowledge mine.

The last words express all Prospero's old bitterness that Caliban has resisted him and refused to respond to his nurture.[1] Indeed, Prospero does not change fundamentally during the play, though, like Samson's, his own accomplished regeneration is put to the test. If he had seriously intended vengeance, why should he have stopped

[1] See the admirable discussion of 'nature' and 'nurture' in *The Tempest* in Middleton Murry's *Shakespeare*, pp. 396 ff.

Sebastian and Antonio murdering Alonso? That he did stop them is proof of his already achieved regeneration from vengeance to mercy. This act, and his talk to Ariel of taking part with his reason against his fury, are once again a re-enactment of a process now past, perhaps extending over a period of many years. I do not wish to imply that the re-enactment is weak or that the temptation to vengeance was not there all the time. Prospero's fury at the thought of Caliban's conspiracy, which interrupts the masque, must be allowed full weight. It is not for nothing that Miranda says that—

> never till this day
> Saw I him touch'd with anger so distemper'd.

We must believe that Prospero felt thus, partly because Caliban's conspiracy typifies all the evil of the world which has so perplexed him, and partly because he is still tempted to be revenged on Alonso and Antonio. He means to pardon them, and he will pardon them. But beneath his reason's sway is this anger against them, which, like Satan's before the sun in *Paradise Lost*, disfigures his face. When Dover Wilson calls Prospero

> a terrible old man, almost as tyrannical and irascible as Lear at the opening of his play,

he makes a valuable comparison, but it should concern Prospero as he once was, not the character who meets us in the play, in whom these traits are mere survivals.

The advantage of this technique of re-enactment was economy, its drawback an inevitable blurring of the sharp outline. The theme of destruction, though exquisitely blended in the whole, is less vivid than it is in *The Winter's Tale*. Having made it so vivid in that play,

54

Shakespeare was probably well content to put the stress on the theme of re-creation. And here he did not work solely by re-enactment. He strengthened Prospero's re-enacted regeneration by the figures of Ferdinand and Miranda. I argued above that, in view of his background of Elizabethan chivalrous convention, Ferdinand need not have been as insignificant as he is usually supposed. Similarly, Miranda's character has been unduly diminished in recent years. To-day, under the stress of the new psychology, men have become nervous lest they should be caught illicitly attaching their daydreams of the perfect woman to a character in fiction. They laugh at the Victorians for falling unawares into this error, and Miranda may have been one of the most popular victims. Hence the anxiety not to admire her too much. E. K. Chambers has written:

> Unless you are sentimentalist inveterate, your emotions will not be more than faintly stirred by the blameless loves at first sight of Ferdinand and Miranda.

Schücking[1] goes further and considers Miranda a poor imitation of Beaumont and Fletcher's idea of the chaste female, an idea that could be dwelt on so lovingly and emphatically only in a lascivious age. In depicting her with her talk of 'modesty, the jewel in my dower' and her protests that if Ferdinand will not marry her, 'I'll die your maid,' and in making Prospero so insistent that she should not lose her maidenhead before marriage, Shakespeare, according to Schücking, is yielding to the demands of his age against his own better judgment. But Miranda is sufficiently successful a symbolic figure

E   [1] *Op. cit.*, pp. 249-50.

for it to matter little if she makes conventional and, in her, unnatural remarks. And even this defence may be superfluous. Since Miranda had never seen a young man, it might reasonably be doubted whether she would behave herself with entire propriety when she did. Prospero, too, had made enough mistakes in his life to be very careful to make no more. Further, Miranda was the heiress to the Duchy of Milan and her father hoped she would be Queen of Naples. What most strikingly emerged from the abdication of our late King was the strong 'anthropological' feeling of the masses of the people concerning the importance of virginity in a King's consort. The Elizabethans were not less superstitious than ourselves and would have sympathised with Prospero's anxiety that the future Queen of Naples should keep her maidenhead till marriage: otherwise ill luck would be sure to follow.

To revert to Miranda's character, like Perdita she is both symbol and human being, yet in both capacities somewhat weaker. She is the symbol of 'original virtue,' like Perdita, and should be set against the devilish figure of Antonio. She is the complete embodiment of sympathy with the men she thinks have been drowned: and her instincts are to create, to mend the work of destruction she has witnessed. She is—again like Perdita, though less clearly—a symbol of fertility. Stephano asks of Caliban, 'Is it so brave a lass?' and Caliban answers,

> Ay, lord; she will become thy bed, I warrant,
> And bring thee forth brave brood.

Even if *The Tempest* was written for some great wedding, it need not be assumed that the masque was inserted merely to fit the occasion. Like the goddesses in Perdita's speeches about the flowers, Juno and Ceres and the song they sing may be taken to reinforce the fertility symbolism embodied in Miranda:

> *Juno.* Honour, riches, marriage-blessing,
> Long continuance, and increasing,
> Hourly joys be still upon you!
> Juno sings her blessings on you.

> *Cer.* Earth's increase, foison plenty,
> Barns and garners never empty,
> Vines with clustering bunches growing,
> Plants with goodly burthen bowing;

> Spring come to you at the farthest
> In the very end of harvest!
> Scarcity and want shall shun you;
> Ceres' blessing so is on you.

The touches of ordinary humanity in Miranda—her siding with Ferdinand against a supposedly hostile father, for instance—are too well known to need recalling. They do not amount to a very great deal and leave her vaguer as a human being than as a symbol. Middleton Murry is not at his happiest when he says that 'they are so terribly, so agonizingly real, these women of Shakespeare's last imagination.' As far as Miranda is concerned, any agonizing sense of her reality derives from the critic and not from the play. But this does not mean that, judged by the play's requirements (which are not those of brilliant realism), Miranda is not perfection. Had she been more weakly drawn, she would have been insignificant, had she been more strongly, she would have interfered with the unifying dominance of Prospero.

Not only do Ferdinand and Miranda sustain Prospero in representing a new order of things that has evolved out of destruction; they also vouch for its continuation. At the end of the play Alonso and Prospero are old and worn men. A younger and happier generation is needed to secure the new state to which Prospero has so painfully brought himself, his friends, and all his enemies save Caliban.

III. PLANES OF REALITY

i. Introductory

I SAID that we ran the risk of being drugged by the heavy enchantments of Prospero's island and hence of missing some of *The Tempest's* significance. But I did not mean that those enchantments could be discounted. To discount the elements of fantasy and remoteness that pervade all three of the plays under discussion and to confine them to the working out of a tragic pattern would be the blindest simplification. And to do so would be to deny flatly a set of responses to the plays so strong and persistent that it cannot but contain a large measure of truth. However prone the less strenuous, that is the more numerous, readers may be to welcome the poetry of fantasy, of 'escape,' and to ignore the sterner kind that deals with life's ultimate problems, they cannot be wholly wrong in enjoying these plays for the idyllic scenes in the Welsh mountains, or pastoral Bohemia, or indeterminate island 'full of noises, sounds, and sweet airs, that give delight and hurt not.' That these scenes exist, and that they go beyond the requirements of any purely tragic pattern, cannot be ignored; their interpretation brings me to the second topic of my essay.

I must repudiate, first of all, any explanation of this idyllic element as fortuitous or trivial: such explanations as that Shakespeare was merely pleasing the fugitive and accidental tastes of his audience or was trying to escape more serious thoughts. It may indeed well be that he had in mind the growing taste for masques and spectacle; but no more in his last than in his previous plays did the public appetite, to which he certainly paid heed, compromise his personal, artistic necessities. Reference to his audience, here as always, leaves the main problem untouched. And, although the idyllic element was not strictly necessary for his particular working out of the tragic pattern in his last plays, it was not hostile to the spirit that prompted him to work out that pattern. Indeed, I believe he treated tragic and idyllic elements with equal seriousness. And there is another resemblance between these two. Just as Shakespeare deals with the already exploited tragic theme in a new way, so he gives a new meaning to idyllic elements which are not lacking in his earlier work. On the other hand, whereas he completed a tragic pattern most of which he had already worked out, he had in treating the idyllic elements a preponderatingly new work to do. And that work was to express something that can be vaguely called metaphysical, some sense of the complexity of existence, of the different planes on which human life can be lived.

And here, once again, I must apologise for some remarks, necessary in their context, whose extreme obviousness makes me ashamed to pronounce them. Most people get a sense of pleasant and reassuring solidity from their everyday occupations. If their nerves are in good order, they find such acts as buying writing-paper, catching a train, or answering an invitation, to be parts of a substantial core of existence. Virginia Woolf has summed up this state of things with perfect vividness and conciseness in the words, 'Tuesday follows

Monday.' Here is the passage from *The Waves* in which the words occur:

> Life is pleasant. Life is good. The mere process of life is satisfactory. Take the ordinary man in good health. He likes eating and sleeping. He likes the snuff of fresh air and walking at a brisk pace down the Strand. Or in the country there's a cock crowing on a gate; there's a foal galloping round a field. Something always has to be done next. Tuesday follows Monday; Wednesday Tuesday. Each spreads the same ripple of well-being, repeats the same curve of rhythm; covers fresh sand with a chill or ebbs a little slackly without. So the being grows rings; identity becomes robust. What was fiery and furtive like a fling of grain cast into the air and blown hither and thither by wild gusts of life from every quarter is now methodical and orderly and flung with a purpose—so it seems.
>
> Lord, how pleasant! Lord, how good! How tolerable is the life of little shopkeepers, I would say, as the train drew through the suburbs and one saw lights in bedroom windows. Active, energetic as a swarm of ants, I said, as I stood at the window and watched workers, bag in hand, stream into town. What hardness, what energy and violence of limb, I thought, seeing men in white drawers scouring after a football on a patch of snow in January.

It cannot be doubted that Shakespeare, with his eye for detail and his healthily slow development, fully shared this way of feeling. Nor did he ever lose it or in any way despise it. These everyday occupations can be gone through with different degrees of intensity, but as long as they appear 'solid,' we are inhabiting the same plane of reality. There are, however, times when in the realm of action even the simplest and the most normal people find their scale of reality upset. Under the stress of war, or love, or a strong disappointment, the things that seemed solid, the acts that seemed to proceed so naturally and without question from one's will, appear remote. Eating and buying writing-paper become rather ridiculous acts which you watch yourself, or rather yourself appearing not yourself, proceeding to do. Santayana has described his hero in *The Last Puritan* falling out of the normal planes of reality:

> A curious film of unreality and worthlessness now seemed to spread over his daily life. Even school work, when he took it up again, occupied him only north-north-west. When the wind was southerly there was a strange void in his bosom. He understood now the old notion that the soul had had previous lives, and was not really at home in this world. The routine of the day seemed a fiction to which he condescended, as if he were playing in private theatricals. The characters were assumed, and not very well done; yet, you must pretend to be in dead earnest, till you actually forgot that you were not. But for him a trap door had opened into the cellarage of this world's stage, which other people seemed so strangely ready to tread all their life long as if it were the bedrock of nature. Yet every step you took on those shaky boards revealed some old folly, some ramshackle contrivance which once may have produced conviction in children watching a Christmas pantomime— children who long since had died of old age. And in the opposite quarter, aloft amid those tall hangings and dingy backdrops, a ray of sunlight had pierced. It had gilded a beam of atoms in the thick dust he had been unconsciously breathing: it had disenchanted the pasteboard castles and daubed forests of his artificial world.

And this is how Virginia Woolf describes the precariousness of our so-called normal equipoise:

One fills up the little compartments of one's engagement book with dinner at eight; luncheon at one-thirty. One has shirts, socks, ties laid out on one's bed.

But it is a mistake, this extreme precision, this orderly and military progress; a convenience, a lie. There is always deep below it, even when we arrive punctually at the appointed time with our white waistcoats and polite formalities, a rushing stream of broken dreams, nursery rhymes, street cries, half-finished sentences and sights—elm trees, willow trees, gardeners sweeping, women writing—that rise and sink even as we hand a lady down to dinner. While one straightens the fork so precisely on the table-cloth, a thousand faces mop and mow.

Once that equipoise is disturbed, the real things are not everyday acts but passionate mental activities. Most people experience this kind of reality at certain moments of their lives. Then there are the states which the average person does not share. There is, for instance, the paranoiac state where all acts and thoughts are judged by reference to a single notion. And there are the states of contemplation, in which all forms of action, all forms of seeking a goal, appear wraithlike and bloodless.

No great poet can be unaware of these and other planes of reality, and in one way or another he has to make his peace with them. In the eighteenth century a poet liked to pretend that things were simpler than without prejudice he would have found them; with the result that Blake, in revolt against his age, passionately protests his own fourfold vision. Perhaps the normal poetic method is to strive to give some sort of unity to whatever planes of reality are apprehended. Something of this sort may be found in *A Midsummer Night's Dream*. Here are presented sets of people whose sense of the normal must in some degree differ: royalty and rustics, lovers and fairies. And the whole play is devoted to creating kinship between the different sets. Bottom in his own way is as much a prince as Theseus; the fairies, for all their exemption from certain human limitations, are as subject to human frailty as mankind. And in the end Shakespeare views the whole problem from the comic, the social point of view. There are many different realities and we may make excursions into them; but the light of common day is sweet and healthy, let us view things in it. Such, anyhow, is the tenor of Theseus's famous comment, too often quoted without the essential final couplet.

> *Hippolyta.* 'Tis strange, my Theseus, that these lovers speak of.
> *Theseus.* More strange than true: I never may believe
> > Those antique fables, nor these fairy toys.
> > Lovers and madmen have such seething brains,
> > Such shaping fantasies, that apprehend
> > More than cool reason ever comprehends.
> > The lunatic, the lover, and the poet
> > Are of imagination all compact:
> > One sees more devils than vast hell can hold;
> > That is the madman: the lover, all as frantic,
> > Sees Helen's beauty in a brow of Egypt:
> > The poet's eye, in a fine frenzy rolling,
> > Doth glance from heaven to earth, from earth to heaven;
> > And, as imagination bodies forth
> > The forms of things unknown, the poet's pen
> > Turns them to shapes and gives to airy nothing
> > A local habitation and a name.
> > Such tricks hath strong imagination,

PLANES OF REALITY

That, if it would but apprehend some joy,
It comprehends some bringer of that joy;
Or, in the night, imagining some fear,
How easy is a bush supposed a bear!

But if the normal poetic method in dealing with
different planes of reality is to try to unite them by
referring them to a single norm, there is another method:
that of communicating the sense of their existence without arranging them in any pattern of subordination.
From modern literature Virginia Woolf is the obvious
illustration. *The Waves* is her most elaborate presentation of as many planes of reality as possible; as if her
sheer sense of their complexity was what she most urgently
needed to express. In *The Years* she has returned to
a pattern, her norm (as in *The Lighthouse*) being that
heightened form of ordinary life which can at moments
be apprehended by most people. It is not every great
writer who uses both methods. Milton, for instance,
with his persistent idealism, must always strive for a
pattern, however rich his material. But Shakespeare,
characteristically, uses both methods. It has been
recently suggested [1] that in mixing fantasy and gravity
Shakespeare used a similar method at the beginning and
end of his career:

The plot of *Love's Labour's Lost* is really over before the
last act begins, and yet it is this last act which is the justification
of the play: a most beautiful piece of decoration and yet in
some mysterious way by no means irrelevant, but a consummation and summary of all that has happened before. It is purely

[1] In the leading article of the *Times Literary Supplement,* August 7th,
1937, *Modern Poetic Drama.*

65

fantastic, with the most rapid and impossible changes from grave poetry to grotesque parody, from high and austere sentiment to mocking and irresponsible humour, and with its various transitions brought about by abrupt and recklessly casual devices. What could be more extraordinary than the messenger of death, unexplained and unprepared, who speaks one word and so changes in a moment the whole mood of the play?

Shakespeare must have been burdened and bewildered, or astonished, or delighted by his sense of life's complexity, at more than one period of his career; and it may well be that in the last act of *Love's Labour's Lost* he was expressing this bewilderment and delight. At other times he felt more confidence, a greater desire to arrange, and he allowed one plane to dominate the rest. In *A Midsummer Night's Dream*, as we saw, and in most of the tragedies Shakespeare at least seeks for unity. However, in *Julius Caesar*, Brutus's type of reality is alien to that of any other person's and is set against it, without being strong enough quite to dominate; it does not become the norm:

> Since Cassius first did whet me against Caesar,
> I have not slept.
> Between the acting of a dreadful thing
> And the first motion, all the interim is
> Like a phantasma, or a hideous dream.

The phantasma is private to Brutus, a realm of life quite distinct from the material portents that frighted Rome on the night before the murder. In *Troilus and Cressida*, too, there is more than one world: a terrible picture of conflicting and never reconciled worlds. Still, this is exceptional, and, up to *Antony and Cleopatra*, the theme of different worlds is not the dominant theme; and when it does come in, the tendency is to unify by making it strictly subordinate. *Antony and Cleopatra* is once again a transitional play. Shakespeare no longer seeks to unify, rather he seeks to emphasise by juxtaposition those worlds which once he had ventured to arrange. *Antony and Cleopatra*, as I explained above, is neither the tragedy nor the triumph of the pair of lovers, it is both simultaneously though on different planes of reality.

In his last three plays Shakespeare was more exercised in his mind by the complexity of possible worlds than at any other period of his working career, and he tried to express his sense of that complexity. Also, from the time of *Antony and Cleopatra* on, this sense was enriched through a new proneness to contemplation. Whether his retirement to Stratford was cause or effect it is idle to ask, but that it was in some way connected can hardly be doubted. Anyhow, although, as we saw in discussing the tragic portion of *The Tempest's* plot, Shakespeare could be at the very heart of action if he wished, he can also see it in an entirely new and mitigating light, like Lucretius's imagined landsman watching at a distance the sailor fighting the storm.

To speak of planes of reality in expressing a common feeling about Shakespeare's last plays has the merit of being simple and unpretentious and of avoiding at once the largely vague and the too cocksurely precise. It implies a state of mind akin to the religious; for simply to present different planes of reality without imposing a pattern on them is an act of homage to the unknown, of humility, the very reverse of self-assertion. But it need not imply any act of religious surrender, any *credo quia non intelligo*. A sense of different planes of reality also renders probable a certain amount of symbolism. The method Shakespeare used in dealing with experience when he arranged it by a consistent norm was not likely to remain valid for his new needs; and if he had hitherto been mainly realistic, he was now likely to supplement realism with symbolism. But again we need not postulate an elaborate repertory of precise symbols. On the other hand, in speaking of planes of reality, we are free either to remain sceptical or to attach to Shakespeare what religious dogmatism or scheme of esoteric significance we happen to fancy. We run fewer risks if we remain sceptical. And that we should hail Shakespeare as familiar with many planes of reality and gifted incomparably with the power of passing from one to another is no slight tribute to him as a poet; and that we should see that power manifested pre-eminently in his last plays is no slight tribute to those plays. Our scepticism runs no risk of being derogatory.

ii. Cymbeline

Shakespeare's first attempt to express his urgent sense of the different planes on which life can be lived was not very successful. (And when I say 'attempt,' I do not mean that there was anything deliberate about it.) For it is vain to hold that *Cymbeline* is a clean and satisfactory achievement. On the other hand, I cannot believe that Shakespeare was quite in the dark; or that the fantastic range of style from brilliant realism to the grossest con-

ventionalism and improbability was no more than a
gratuitous and wanton outburst.   One of the best passages
in Granville-Barker's excellent preface to the play is that
in which he insists that the ingenuousnesses are inten-
tional.   Take, for instance, one of the most flagrant
examples: Belarius's informative soliloquy at the end of
the third scene of the third act:

> These boys know little they are sons to the King;
> Nor Cymbeline dreams that they are alive.
> They think they are mine; and though train'd up thus meanly
> I' the cave wherein they bow, their thoughts do hit
> The roofs of palaces, and nature prompts them
> In simple and low things to prince it much
> Beyond the trick of others . . .
> O Cymbeline! heaven and my conscience knows
> Thou didst unjustly banish me: whereon,
> At three and two years old, I stole these babes;
> Thinking to bar thee of succession, as
> Thou reft'st me of my lands.   Euriphile,
> Thou wast their nurse; they took thee for their mother,
> And every day do honour to her grave:
> Myself, Belarius, that am Morgan call'd,
> They take for natural father.

Not only does the soliloquy offend against all probability
as to its utterance, but it is difficult to see how, in his
mountain isolation, Belarius could have known the intimate thoughts of Cymbeline.   Yet that Shakespeare
committed this offence because he was tired or careless
is most difficult to believe.   At the time of *Cymbeline*,
dramatic technique must have been easy to him: in his
sleep or in his cups it would have been easier for him to
devise something more competent.   It is more probable

that the ingenuousness, like that of the Euripidean pro-
logue, was intended.

On the other hand, Granville-Barker may be wrong in
limiting the play to a piece of technical sophistication.
He says, 'Shakespeare has an unlikely story to tell,' and
proceeds to explain, relying especially on the theatrical
conditions, with what artifice he did his job. But to say
'Shakespeare has an unlikely story to tell' is to beg the
main critical question. And this is: why did Shakespeare
choose so unlikely a story? Or, more fully, why did
Shakespeare take the trouble to go to three quite different
originals, thus letting himself in for a dramatic task of
extreme difficulty, which he can perform only by forfeit-
ing the kind of dramatic probability which he normally
accepted? His immediate originals were an Italian
novel, early British history derived from Holinshed, and
a fairy story of the wicked step-mother and innocent
step-daughter. And behind them may be the general
pressure of Sidney's *Arcadia*. Critics have tried to dis-
integrate the play and assign bits away from Shakespeare.
But no one doubts Shakespeare's choice of the three main
motives; and the burden of accounting for that choice
remains. (Personally, in view of the amount of queer-
ness one has to swallow, I can see no reason for not
swallowing the whole, Posthumus's vision included.[1])
Well, did Shakespeare choose the three themes for the
sole reason of setting himself technical problems by
solving which he could exhibit his virtuosity; in par-

[1] G. Wilson Knight, *The Vision of Jupiter in Cymbeline*, in the
Times Literary Supplement, November 21st, 1936, p. 958, argues for
its authenticity. One may accept his conclusion without accepting his
obiter dicta on Shakespeare's last plays.

ticular that he might indulge in the technical debauch of a super-dénouement in the last scene? or had he some other motive? That he enjoyed the debauch need not be denied, but that he went out of his way to amalgamate three plots in order to prepare for it is hard to admit. More likely the wealth of plot-material corresponded to some desire in Shakespeare's mind; and this desire was to express his sense of the different worlds we live in. He attempted to do so by one of the most obvious means: diversity of plot. His attempt was experimental, yet at first serious. It may have become less serious during composition, as Shakespeare felt success eluding him. And he may have been glad to cover his failure with that cloak of artful and pseudo-ingenuous sophistication of which Granville-Barker speaks.

When we call Shakespeare's last plays romances, I suppose we mean that his material is remote and improbable and that he uses the happy ending. It would be more helpful, at least in thinking of *Cymbeline*, to use the word *romance* as Hazlitt did, who thought of this play as a narrative romance adapted to the stage:

> Cymbeline may be considered as a dramatic romance, in which the most striking parts of the story are thrown into the form of a dialogue, and the intermediate circumstances are explained by the different speakers, as occasion renders it necessary. The action is less concentrated in consequence; but the interest becomes more aërial and refined from the principle of perspective introduced into the subject by the imaginary changes of scene, as well as by the length of time it occupies.

It may well be that Hazlitt gives our inquiry the right direction. Turning from Roman history to the romances,

Underdowne's translation of Heliodorus, for instance, or Sidney's *Arcadia*, Shakespeare may have felt that this rich complexity corresponded in some obscure way with what was now occupying his mind. A story told by the author was one thing, but a story within that story, told by a character (a device common to both the above books), was something a little different. And the difference may have interested him. The general effect, too, of the rapidly changing incidents, the extraordinary accidents, the mixture of improbability with moral wisdom would express a sense of wonder, of the strange mix-up of things, that would easily provide a correlative to a newly sharpened sense of the many planes on which life could be lived. Thus, attracted by the implications of the romance, Shakespeare in *Cymbeline* attempts to imitate the diversity of its material and the surprising turns of its plot.

In the previous chapter I spoke of realism and symbolism in the characters, but I did not say why Shakespeare chose to blend them in a way hitherto unpractised by him. There was no absolute need, in expressing the last part of the tragic pattern, to depart from the realistic methods of the tragedies proper, even though it may have been convenient to mark off the theme of re-creation from that of destruction by a change of manner. But by adding variety of character-treatment to variety of plot, Shakespeare could powerfully enrich his means of expressing his sense of different worlds. And this was the main reason for his new treatment of character.

In addition to these contrasts, there is a new contrast of style, tending to express the same things. The packed, arduous, stormy, and eminently dramatic verse of the late tragedies is still there. Take Iachimo's first speeches aiming at the seduction of Imogen:

> What, are men mad? Hath nature given them eyes
> To see this vaulted arch, and the rich crop
> Of sea and land, which can distinguish 'twixt
> The fiery orbs above and the twinn'd stones
> Upon the number'd beach? and can we not
> Partition make with spectacles so precious
> 'Twixt fair and foul?

Imo. What makes your admiration?

Iach. It cannot be i' the eye, for apes and monkeys
> 'Twixt two such shes would chatter this way and
> Contemn with mows the other; nor i' the judgement,
> For idiots in this case of favour would
> Be wisely definite; nor i' the appetite;
> Sluttery to such neat excellence opposed
> Should make desire vomit emptiness,
> Not so allured to feed.

Imo. What is the matter, trow?

Iach. The cloyed will,
> That satiate yet unsatisfied desire, that tub
> Both filled and running, ravening first the lamb,
> Longs after for the garbage.

But another music, remote, unearthly, slow, and not very dramatic, first detected in *Pericles*, now appears in palpable contrast. It marks especially the scenes in the Welsh mountains. This is how Guiderius and Arviragus describe their life.

Gui. We, poor unfledged,
> Have never wing'd from view o' the nest, nor know not
> What air's from home. Haply this life is best,
> If quiet life be best; sweeter to you

73

That have a sharper known; well corresponding
With your stiff age: but unto us it is
A cell of ignorance; travelling a-bed;
A prison for a debtor, that not dares
To stride a limit.

Arv.   What should we speak of
When we are old as you? when we shall hear
The rain and wind beat dark December, how,
In this our pinching cave, shall we discourse
The freezing hours away? We have seen nothing;
We are beastly, subtle as the fox for prey,
Like warlike as the wolf for what we eat;
Our valour is to chase what flies; our cage
We make a quire, as doth the prison'd bird,
And sing our bondage freely.

If this type of music was confined to *Cymbeline*, we might infer that it exists for no more than to depict the remote life of Belarius and the boys in the Welsh mountains: unspoilt nature set against the broken and hectic life of the court. But it occurred in *Pericles* and was to occur in the two later plays; hence it can hardly not have a more general significance. And it implies a way of feeling about life. Through this unearthly music Shakespeare expresses a feeling of seeing life distanced, instead of identifying himself with whatever action is being transacted.

The chief merit of *Cymbeline* as a stage play is its liveliness. There is a constant and diversified stream of interesting incident, fluctuating in intensity of feeling and in its kinship to tragedy, comedy, farce, or romance. It is extremely agreeable and diverting to watch. And Shakespeare's sure general grasp of this miscellany arouses

74

in us the zest of admiration. It cannot be said that Shakespeare's sense of different worlds, however important a part of the meaning, is conveyed strongly by the whole play. He did not put his various means of conveying that meaning to any very skilful use. The diversity of plot causes confusion rather than contrast. Realism and symbolism in Imogen's character do the same. The changes of style are far more effective, but there is little apparent reason for their occurrence. Shakespeare is apt to maintain one kind of style so long that he accustoms us to it thoroughly enough to make us take it for granted. For instance, the scene of Imogen's burial is drawn out: we are satisfied with it, and when she wakes with the words, 'Yes, sir, to Milford-Haven,' there is no shock of surprise, as there might have been if the burial scene had left us hungry and wanting more. On the other hand, the brisk and business-like entry of Lucius and the Romans after Imogen's strained, moving, and melodramatic soliloquy over Cloten's body is the effective breaking-in of one world on another. Imogen, addressing the body she supposes to be Posthumus's and falling on it, says:

> Give colour to my pale cheek with thy blood,
> That we the horrider may seem to those
> Which chance to find us: O, my lord, my lord.

> *Enter* Lucius, *a* Captain *and other* Officers, *and a* Soothsayer.

Cap. To them the legions garrison'd in Gallia,
    After your will, have cross'd the sea, attending
    You here at Milford-Haven with your ships:
    They are in readiness.

But on the whole, Shakespeare's attempt in *Cymbeline* to convey his feeling of different planes of reality ends in the queer phantasmagoric effect of a welter of unreality rather than in a vision of those different planes standing out in sharp and thrilling contrast.

iii. The Winter's Tale

If *The Winter's Tale* succeeded better than *Cymbeline* with the tragic pattern, so did it with the planes of reality also. No blurring, but clean contrast. The paranoiac world of Leontes is set against the everyday world of the courtiers and the world, still of everyday but intensified, of Hermione. Leontes's world is marvellously expressed by the hot and twisted language he uses. Another world is introduced at the beginning of the third act by the short scene where Cleomenes and Dion speak of their visit to the Oracle. Here the words are cool and pellucid: we are in the realm of contemplation.

> *Cleo.* The climate's delicate, the air most sweet,
> Fertile the isle, the temple much surpassing
> The common praise it bears.
> *Dion.*   I shall report,
> For most it caught me, the celestial habits,
> Methinks I so should term them, and the reverence
> Of the grave wearers. O, the sacrifice!
> How ceremonious, solemn, and unearthly
> It was i' the offering.

And this 'ceremonious, solemn, and unearthly' note is repeated in the great scene, in itself fantastically unreal where Leontes views Hermione's statue and it comes to life. It would be tedious to speak of every transition in this play from one world to another. I will confine myself to noting the most violent of all, and one which the greatest sceptic of my argument would hardly consider accidental. Antigonus, on the coast of Bohemia, carrying the infant Perdita, sends the mariner back to his ship and proceeds to describe in a soliloquy how Hermione appeared to him in a dream. There is nothing in the play so melodramatic, so remote from ordinary life as this speech:

> She did approach
> My cabin where I lay; thrice bow'd before me,
> And gasping to begin some speech, her eyes
> Became two spouts: the fury spent, anon
> Did this break from her—

and when she had done speaking, 'with shrieks she melted into air.' From this strained, impossible world we are abruptly recalled by the stage direction *exit, pursued by a bear*, and the entry of the old shepherd, whose first words put us at the very centre of common humanity:

> I would there were no age between ten and three-and-twenty, or that youth would sleep out the rest; for there is nothing in the between but getting wenches with child, wronging the ancientry, stealing, fighting.

It is worth noting, in parenthesis, that the above abrupt transition not only expresses the sense of different worlds but has an important technical work to do, that of throwing a bridge across the two halves of the play. Shakespeare has to present us in the country scenes with a new

77

kind of serious writing, with re-creation after destruction. Now it is easy enough to set the farcical or the grotesque against tragedy without fear of misunderstanding. But to set the serious world of Perdita abruptly against the other serious world of Leontes and Hermione might make trouble. Perdita might appear too slight, set against the earlier violence. Shakespeare's solution is to drive the tortured world of Leontes and Hermione to a ridiculous extreme in Antigonus's vision. In so doing he really puts an end to it. Any return to it would court ridicule. But the ridiculousness of Antigonus's vision prepares us for any kind of the ridiculous; and Shakespeare proceeds to give us good earthy comedy, and we take it. Out of this comedy grows the serious, sane, and transfigured earthiness of the Perdita scenes, which we now never dream of confusing with the world of Leontes and Hermione. This transition has obvious analogies with music.

iv. The Tempest

Speaking of planes of reality in terms of colour, we can say: that in *Cymbeline* there are many colours but that they have run and are blurred; that in *The Winter's Tale* they are set one against another in striking and successful contrast; and that in *The Tempest* the colours are broken into a brilliant pattern, very complicated, yet not confused, a pattern consisting of large bold contrasts, of small subtle contrasts, and of delicate transitions. Nor is the sense of planes of reality fitful; it permeates the entire play and is, indeed, its main motive. Expressed so superlatively well, it contributes very largely to the

unexhausted freshness of the play at every reading. A
few examples of contrast or transition must suffice.

In the first act two storms are described, and through
them two worlds. The first is presented on the stage
with the utmost realism; the second is narrated as if it
were a fairy tale: an impossible vessel, an impossibly
contented baby, and winds that sympathised with their
freight:

Prospero.   They hurried us aboard a bark,
  Bore us some leagues to sea; where they prepared
  A rotten carcase of a butt, not rigg'd,
  Nor tackle, sail, nor mast; the very rats
  Instinctively have quit it: there they hoist us,
  To cry to the sea that roar'd to us, to sigh
  To the winds whose pity, sighing back again,
  Did us but loving wrong.
Miranda.   Alack, what trouble
  Was I then to you!
Pros.   O, a cherubin
  Thou wast that didst preserve me. Thou didst smile,
  Infused with a fortitude from heaven,
  When I have deck'd the sea with drops full salt,
  Under my burthen groan'd.

In the third scene of the third act Antonio and Sebastian
agree to hold to their plot against Alonso in spite of the
rebuff they have had; and immediately after this piece of
tragic actuality comes the strange music, the banquet, and
Ariel's entrance as a harpy. In Ariel's song the homeli-
ness of the watch-dogs and of the cock cuts across the
fairy remoteness of the rest. In *A Midsummer Night's
Dream* Shakespeare had approximated his sprites and his
human beings; in *The Tempest* he keeps them to their

own worlds. Caliban is intractable to human civility; Ariel can feel pity only at a remove, by an effort of analogy, and is ever fretting to break his bonds to a man and be free in his own element. But the most complicated display of different worlds occurs in the fourth act. First, there is the betrothal of Ferdinand and Miranda, a piece of ordinary life much stylised in the execution; then follows the masque, in itself a simple piece of make-believe. Into these tranquil worlds of convention and make-believe breaks the realism of Caliban's plot, while Prospero's 'Our revels now are ended' suddenly distances all these worlds into a common unreality. When we examine the masque, we find that, though its function may be simple, the means by which it is presented are complicated in a manner we associate rather with Pirandello than with the Elizabethan drama. On the actual stage the masque is executed by players pretending to be spirits, pretending to be real actors, pretending to be supposed goddesses and rustics.

I alluded earlier to Ariel's realistic description of the drunken conspirators approaching Prospero's cell, and said that its occurrence after Prospero's great speech was not fortuitous. Not only does Shakespeare express his sense of different worlds by this arrangement, but he reassures us of the certainty with which he controls his material. That he can pass so easily from one world to the other, without a suspicion of blurring either, proves him still at the height of his powers, in full grasp of life, and, as artist, entire master of what he is doing.

IV. THE RELATION OF THE
TWO THEMES

———————

I HAVE spoken of two large themes in Shakespeare's last plays. The question remains: Does he succeed in making them reinforce each other or do they conflict? *Cymbeline* is so loose that one is hardly conscious of any relation between them; they resemble bodies moving in so wide a space that one has no influence on the other. In *The Winter's Tale* they on the whole reinforce each other. In the tragic pattern exhibited in that play different planes of reality quite naturally occur. Leontes's mania is simultaneously the disintegrating force in the tragic plot and a world different from any other world in the play. Antigonus's dream and the old shepherd's entry are at least as important to the plot-mechanism of the tragic pattern as to showing contrasted states of being. The trance-like reunion of Leontes and Hermione both supplements the theme of reconstruction and creates the sense of the contemplative life. But even if the themes co-operate, it is the tragic theme that gives the play its main outline. And it may be that Shakespeare presented the different planes of reality in fairly large and simple contrasts, in order that the reader might not be tempted to dwell on them too long but could easily keep them subordinate to the tragic pattern. Anyhow, if both themes had been equipollent, the sense of unity must have been disturbed.

In *The Tempest*, Shakespeare's desire for unity was peremptory. Within the tragic pattern, he forsook the method he had used in *The Winter's Tale*, of juxtaposing the themes of destruction and regeneration. Instead, he sunk the main tragic action in the past and brought it into view mainly through the secondary process of re-enactment. Regeneration emerges dominant from the total tragic pattern. He did something of the same sort in arranging his different worlds. If in *The Winter's Tale* these are presented without comment, in *The Tempest*, however vividly he keeps his worlds apart, he does, in the interests of unity, imply a subordination. For, however vivid the realistic elements may be, the fact remains that in the final view they sink a little into the background, and the general impression of the play is that of remoteness. As we read or witness them, those elements do indeed come to the fore, but only to sink back into the vaguer general impression. The paradox meets us at the very beginning. In a way, the shipwreck is highly realistic, and it serves with brilliant economy to bring out the characters of the actors. Yet we soon feel that it is a manipulated shipwreck, which we watch rather than share. (Nugent Monck had the right instinct when he put Prospero and Miranda on the stage from the beginning and thus persuaded the audience to see the shipwreck partly through their eyes.) Shakespeare has, in fact, adjusted the balance sufficiently but with infinite delicacy on the side of contemplation, causing us to see what is in itself truly tragic or truly paradoxical through the philosophical eyes of Prospero. Thus it is that the most famous speech of the play does give a unity to it. Not that it in the least sums the play up; rather it is like evening sunlight sending its beams on objects very varied and unlike itself, yet fusing them in a common illumination. The 'cloud-capp'd towers,' then, and the rest are the culmination of the play. And not only does contemplation give unity to the planes of reality expressed, but it is strong enough to tone down the other theme, the tragic pattern, into subordination to itself. Even the theme of regeneration, the most powerfully developed portion of the tragic pattern, must in the end take a second place in the total ordering of the play. But, though Shakespeare may have arranged his material in the above pattern, he did not abandon the method, used in *The Winter's Tale*, of making one feature serve two turns. Antonio and Sebastian, for instance, present the destructive portion of the tragic pattern, and at the same time a world that stands sharply contrasted to most others in the play. Miranda, symbol of regeneration, sees as a 'brave, new world' something which to the other characters wears a very different aspect.

V. EPILOGUE

IT may be that in his last plays Shakespeare was trying to express more than ever before, which of course does not mean that he actually did express more. But he had not apparently tried before to unite the mainly human theme of tragedy with the theme of planes of reality tending to the religious. It is almost as if he aimed at rendering the complete theme of *The Divine Comedy*. Indeed, it is not fantastic to see in *The Winter's Tale* Shakespeare's attempt to compress that whole theme into a single play through the direct presentation of all its parts: and it was with this notion in mind that I spoke of the country scenes as an earthly paradise. The motives of hell and purgatory in Leontes are obvious enough, while the statue scene is conducted in a rarefied atmosphere of contemplation that suggests the motive of paradise. I do not wish to press the Dantesque analogy, but would rather end my remarks on *The Winter's Tale* by saying: the play includes so much and does such relative justice to what it includes, that it must sacrifice some strength to its other virtues. It is as good as it can be in the circumstances, and one of Shakespeare's masterpieces.

In *The Tempest*, Shakespeare, though nominally including the whole of the matter of *The Winter's Tale*, did, as we saw, subordinate certain things, especially the destructive part of the tragic pattern and the realism that usually accompanies it. *The Winter's Tale* tries to sum up all, doing equal justice to all. In *The Tempest*, Shakespeare forgoes such justice and subordinates to his newest state of mind those qualities he had already presented in earlier plays. In so doing, he expressed that state of mind more completely and more intensely than before. And, in a way, he knit *The Tempest* more closely to his earlier work. Being all-inclusive and doing justice to what it includes, *The Winter's Tale* stands by itself, a microcosm. *The Tempest* is not meant to endure such a degree of isolation. Through his method of re-enacting or recalling and not fully stating the element of destruction, Shakespeare implies that he is partly relying on his previous fuller statement of it. He would have us cast our minds back. Thus, however much else *The Tempest* means, a part of its meaning consists in its final, supplementary function. Not only does it give Shakespeare's fullest sense of the different worlds we can inhabit; it is also the necessary epilogue to an already apprehended series of tragic masterpieces.